Henrietta B. Seiberling
Ohio's Lady with a Cause

AF799830

Dick B.'s Reference Titles on Alcoholics Anonymous History

Paradise Research Publications, Inc., Publisher;
Good Book Publishing Company, Distributor P.O. Box 837, Kihei, HI 96753-0837
Phone/Fax: (808) 874 4876; Email: dickb@dickb.com; URL: http://www.dickb.com/index.shtml

Publisher's December 1, 2005 List of Titles by Author Dick B.; All list prices: Effective December 1, 2005

Anne Smith's Journal, 1933-1939, 3rd ed.; 1998; 6 x 9; 180 pp.; $16.95

By the Power of God: A Guide to Early A.A. Groups & Forming Similar Groups Today; 2000, 6 x 9; 260 pp., $16.95

Cured!: Proven Help for Alcoholics and Addicts; 2003, 6 x 9; 182 pp., $17.95

Dr. Bob and His Library, 3rd ed.; 1998; 6 x 9; 156 pp.; $15.95

God and Alcoholism: Our Growing Opportunity in the 21st Century; 2002; 6 x 9; 190 pp.; $17.95

Good Morning!: Quiet Time, Morning Watch, Meditation, and Early A.A.; 2d ed.; 1998; 6 x 9; 154 pp.; $16.95

Henrietta B. Seiberling: Ohio's Lady with a Cause, 4th ed. 2006; 6 x 9; $15.95

Making Known The Biblical History and Roots of Alcoholics Anonymous: An Eleven-Year Research, Writing, Publishing and Fact Dissemination Project, ed. 2005 6 x 9; $19.95

New Light on Alcoholism: God, Sam Shoemaker, and A.A.; 2d ed.; 1999; 6 x 9; 672 pp.; $24.95

The Akron Genesis of Alcoholics Anonymous, 2d ed.; 1998; 6 x 9; 400 pp.; $17.95

The Books Early AAs Read for Spiritual Growth, 7th ed.; 1998; 6 x 9; 126 pp.; $15.95

The First Nationwide A.A. History Conference - Comments of Dick B., 2003, 8 ½ x 11, 79 pp., spiral bound, $17.95

The Golden Text of A.A.: God, the Pioneers, and Real Spirituality; 1999; 6 x 9; 76 pp.; $14.95

The Good Book and The Big Book: A.A.'s Roots in the Bible; 2d ed.; 1997; 6 x 9; 264 pp.; $17.95

The James Club: The Original A.A. Program's Absolute Essentials, 3rd ed., 2005; 6 x 9; $17.95

The Oxford Group & Alcoholics Anonymous, 2d ed.; 1998; 6 x 9; 432 pp.; $17.95

That Amazing Grace (Clarence & Grace S.); 1996; 6 x 9; 160 pp.; $16.95

Turning Point: A History of Early A.A.'s Spiritual Roots and Successes; 1997; 6 x 9; 776 pp.; $29.95

Twelve Steps for You: Let Our Creator, A.A. History, and the Big Book Be Your Guide; 2003; 6 x 9; 90 pp. $17.95

Utilizing Early A.A.'s Spiritual Roots for Recovery Today; Rev. ed.; 1999; 6 x 9; 106 pp., $14.95

When Early AA s Were Cured and Why; 2d ed. 2005, 6 x 9; $17.95

Why Early A.A. Succeeded: The Good Book in Alcoholics Anonymous Yesterday and Today (a Bible Study Primer), 2001; 6 x 9; 340 pp., $17.95

Available through other distributors

Hope: The Story of Geraldine O. Delaney, 2d ed. NJ: Alina Lodge

Our Faith Community A.A. Legacy (Dick B., ed and compiler). FL: Came to Believe Publications

Courage to Change (with Bill Pittman). MN: Hazelden

Women Pioneers of AA (Dick B., contributor). MN: Hazelden

Henrietta B. Seiberling
Ohio's Lady with a Cause

Dick B.
Historian, Bible Student, Retired Attorney, Recovered AA
(Author of 26 Titles on Early A.A.'s Spiritual Roots)

Paradise Research Publications, Inc.
Kihei, Maui, Hawaii

Paradise Research Publications, Inc.
P.O. Box 837
Kihei, HI 96753-0837
(808) 874-4876
Email: dickb@dickb.com
URL: http://www.dickb.com/index.shtml

© 2004, 2005, 2006 by Anonymous.
All rights reserved. Published 2004. 4th Edition 2006

Printed in the United States of America

Cover Design: Terry Dunford (American Creations of Maui)

This Paradise Research Publications Edition is published by arrangement with Good Book Publishing Company, PO Box 837, Kihei, HI: 96753-0837

The publication of this volume does not imply affiliation with, nor approval or endorsement from Alcoholics Anonymous World Services, Inc. The views expressed herein are solely those of the author. A.A. is a program of recovery from alcoholism–use of the Twelve Steps in connection with programs and activities which are patterned after A.A. but which address other problems, does not imply otherwise.

Note: All Bible verses quoted in this book, unless otherwise noted, are from the Authorized (or "King James") Version. The letters "KJV" are used when necessary to distinguish it from other versions.

ISBN: 1-885803-93-1

To The Honorable John F. Seiberling, Former U.S. Congressman from Akron, Ohio

With two of his mother's favorite verses from 1 John 4:20-21 in the Good Book:

> If a man say, I love God, and hateth his brother, he is a liar; for he that loveth not his brother whom he hath seen, how can he love God whom he hath not seen? And this commandment have we from him, That he who loveth God love his brother also.

Contents

Contents

1

A Brief Glance at Henrietta's Life

The story of the rise and decline of the rubber industry in Akron has been told elsewhere. So too the details of the career of Frank A. Seiberling, industrialist, philanthropist, founder of Goodyear Tire and Rubber Company in 1898, and later founder of the Seiberling Rubber Company in the early 1920's. See, for example, Steve Love and David Giffels. *Wheels of Fortune: The Story of Rubber in Akron* (Akron, OH: University of Akron Press, 1999); Mansel G. Blackford and K. Austin Kerr. *B.F. Goodrich: Tradition and Transformation, 1870-1995* (Columbus, OH: Ohio State University Press, 1996); Hugh Allen. *The House of Goodyear: Fifty Years of Men and Industry* (Cleveland, OH: Corday & Gross, 1949); Alfred Lief. *The Firestone Story: a History of the Firestone Tire & Rubber Company* (New York, NY: Whittlesey House, 1951); and Hugh Allen. *Rubber's Home Town: The Real-Life Story of Akron* (New York, NY: Stratford House, 1949).

Henrietta Buckler Seiberling's own story should probably begin with what her son John described to me as the "Goodyear Period" *circa* 1910. For it was then that F.A. Seiberling built his baronial mansion called Stan Hywet Hall. The years 1900 to 1910 had marked the expansion of Goodyear Tire and Rubber Company ("the greatest name in rubber").World War I enhanced the demand for tires; and at the end of that war, F.A. was worth sixty million dollars–the wealthiest man in Akron.

But 1921 saw a recession, and things began to tumble straight through to the industrialist's death in 1959. His huge mansion and beautiful gardens could not be maintained by his family; yet the family did not want to sell. In consequence, all was offered to the community on condition that it make a go of establishing an acquiring non-profit foundation. Also, that title to the Gate Lodge would not pass to that foundation until the end of the joint lives of all the F.A. Seiberling children. An event that recently occurred with the death of Irene Seiberling Harrison who occupied the Lodge from 1960 until her death.

Seiberling's Stan Hywet Hall was one of the largest private residences in Ohio. It still stands as a nonprofit foundation, museum, and National Historic Landmark. The opening of its Gate Lodge in 2004 adds a new dimension to its historical significance.

Now to Henrietta herself.

When I was growing up in the 1930's, Akron's rubber industry was, in my mind, more associated with the Goodyear Blimp and the Firestone Hour, than with the persons of its influential fathers such as Dr. Benjamin Franklin Goodrich, Charles Goodyear, Frank A. Seiberling, Harvey S. Firestone, and Paul W. Litchfield. Moreover, Akron's long and famous association with tires was soon to give place to plant closings. And the rubber era ended when General Tire & Rubber Co. shut down in 1981.

The Seiberling name, however, was destined to live on in Ohio's history books.

To backtrack a bit, John Frederick Seiberling, one of F.A.'s children, had joined the National Guard; gone to the Mexican Border in 1915 to stop Pancho Villa; and met Henrietta Buckler during the war years. John Frederick (called "Fred") married Henrietta Buckler in Akron at Stan Hywet in October, 1917. Fred went overseas; and the first child of the marriage, also named John, was born in September, 1918. Fred became ill with anemic dysentery in 1919 but recovered to face the financial crash and the family's loss of Goodyear. F.A. launched Seiberling Rubber Company, and Fred was made its manager in Newcastle, Pennsylvania. But Fred soon tired of the job and returned to Akron with Henrietta and their (by then) family of three children.

Henrietta could not see bringing up her children in the big Seiberling mansion and moved to the Gate Lodge on the Stan Hywet Hall estate grounds. Fred and Henrietta parted company, separating in 1935; but Henrietta and her three children continued living at the Gate Lodge. In spite, however, of the Fred Seiberling family's ups and downs, life had actually begun rather well for Henrietta Buckler herself.

She was born in Lawrenceburg, Kentucky on March 18, 1888. She was the only child of Judge Julius A. and Mary Maddox Buckler. She grew up in El Paso, Texas where her father was judge of the common pleas court. And later she matriculated at Vassar College where she majored in music and minored in psychology. From that institution she received a B.A. degree.

Let's return to the Seiberling name, and specifically to Henrietta's own family.

After their marriage on September 12, 1917, Fred and Henrietta had three children. Neither Henrietta nor any of her children were alcoholics. John F. Seiberling, Jr., was the oldest Fred Seiberling offspring. He graduated from Harvard College in 1941 and enlisted in the United States Army where he had a distinguished career in the Quartermaster Corps. He became responsible for the solution of many of the Army's transportation challenges and difficulties in Europe and particularly in the Normandy Invasion. John was decorated with the Legion of Merit and later the Bronze Star. He concluded his military service as a Major. He then attended Columbia Law School, worked as Vice President and General Counsel of Goodyear in their law department for 17 years, became a United States Congressman from Akron, and still later director of Akron University's Peace Studies Center. John Jr.'s sisters were Mary Seiberling Huhn, a resident of Devon, Pennsylvania, and Dorothy Seiberling Stiber, who lives in Shelter Island, New York. Both of these Seiberling daughters graduated from Vassar College, as did their mother Henrietta.

Henrietta was a Presbyterian from childhood. She was not an avid churchgoer. But she was an eager and well-versed Bible student and reader. Henrietta was a member of Westminster Presbyterian Church in Akron on West Market Street. The minister was Rev. J. C. Wright; and Henrietta took all her children to Dr. Wright's Presbyterian Church. All three children were baptized there in their teens. And Henrietta and her family often attended this church over a period of several years–the church also being the place of worship for A.A. founder Dr. Robert H. Smith and his wife Anne, who were charter members.

All three of Henrietta's children wrote me quite extensively about their mother. They all greatly admired her, her beliefs, and her principles. Her youngest child, Dorothy Seiberling Stiber, wrote:

> She was a seeker, and it took the form of Christian belief. She had aspirations toward spiritual and moral improvement. By observing and trying to live by the standards of the Oxford Group, she achieved greater humility and surrendered her ego and fears to God.

In one of his many letters to me, son John Seiberling, Jr., wrote:

> Henrietta made a constant effort to lead a life of Christian spirituality and to help others do the same . . . . Humility and the belief that people are more important than things were uppermost in her messages. Also, the importance of being right on the inside, not just the appearance of being right. Her Bible reading and her daily quiet times were an effort to let God guide her life.

John's sister, Mary Seiberling Huhn, wrote:

> Mother became intensely interested in the teachings and story of Jesus. She turned to them for help in her own problems and then was able to use the insights gained as she nurtured the developing AA. Mother was always quoting from the Bible to teach us how to get along better. When we were quarreling or angry and said spiteful things, she would say, 'If you don't love your brother whom you have seen, how can you love God whom you haven't seen?'

Henrietta Buckler Seiberling died in New York City on December 5, 1979. She is buried at Lawrenceburg, Kentucky. And there follows the story of this non-alcoholic woman and her very unusual connection with the founding and development of Alcoholics Anonymous.

2

An Accurate Description of A.A.'s Real Spiritual Roots

The Distorted Historical Picture Today

He who plans to look into the origins of Alcoholics Anonymous will immediately visit a whirlpool of confusion, misinformation, distortion, omission, and opinionated viewpoints. Sad though it seems, A.A.'s real history and spiritual roots began to disappear almost as soon as its basic text *Alcoholics Anonymous* (affectionately called the "Big Book") was published in the Spring of 1939. For some sad reason, these roots continue to be muddied with each new purported history and biography that joins the increasing plethora of stories and opinions.

Confusion over the Date of Founding

The confusion over who did what probably began the moment A.A. was founded. In fact, the very date of its founding was disputed for some years. Today it's Akron date is still in dispute. Lois Wilson, the wife of A.A. co-founder Bill Wilson, insisted A.A. was founded in 1934 when Wilson began bringing drunks to the Wilson home in Brooklyn. Some would think it began when Bill Wilson met Dr. Bob at Henrietta Seiberling's Gate Lodge in Akron in May, 1939. But Bob was still drinking then and returned briefly to drinking thereafter. The founding date seemed fixed at June 10, 1935–the date that Dr. Bob had his last drink. But a few investigators have recently claimed that the June 10th date is wrong. They put Dr. Bob's last drink at another time. Even Bill Wilson himself once proclaimed that the first A.A. *group* was founded after A.A. Number Three (attorney Bill Dotson) was released from the hospital a cured man, just a short time after Bill and Bob began their program. Finally, T. Henry Williams–in whose home the early A.A. members met–frequently claimed it all started when Henrietta Seiberling, a tiny Oxford Group contingent, and Dr. Bob knelt on T. Henry's carpet and prayed for Dr. Bob's healing (See T. Willard Hunter. *"It Started Right*

There" Behind the Twelve Steps and Self-help Movement. Oregon: Grosvenor Books, 1994). This time and place, as we shall see, was before Wilson had met Smith.

I believe the founding date is the least relevant part of our great history and roots. But if it fell to me today to specify the date when A.A. was founded, I would select Mother's Day in 1935 when A.A.'s two founders first met and began their dialogue. This despite the fact that Dr. Bob did go on a short drinking spree thereafter, then to take his last drink on some now disputed date in June, 1935.

Confusion over Which Was the "Original" Program

The real question is where and how did the program itself originate and what were the ingredients of that "original" program. Here again, confusion reigns. The reason is that *three* different programs appeared to be in progress at the time Bill Wilson had published his Big Book in 1939. The first *may* possibly have been a word-of-mouth group of *six* ideas which Wilson described in various ways yet claimed were in common use during the developmental period. The second–quite simply and accurately defined by A.A.'s trustee-to-be Frank Amos for John D. Rockefeller, Jr.–consisted of *seven* points which were used to bring about the cure of forty pioneers by 1938. Yet after Bill had been commissioned by a closely-split vote to write a book that would portray "the" program to all the world, Wilson proceeded to write his Big Book and included *twelve* steps which he curiously claimed "we took" (presumably referring to the pioneers in Akron and New York). See *Alcoholics Anonymous*, 4th ed., p. 59: "Here are the steps we took," said Bill–even though the steps did not exist until after he had written them in late 1938 and published them in 1939.

The Tangled Sources Which Were Involved

For an honest statement of the roots of the A.A. program, one must look to a variety of sources, some of which are in dispute to this very day. Yet no discussion here of Henrietta's role in the great Akron cures would be accurate without looking at the whole picture. That picture necessarily included some medical, psychotherapeutic, and even extra-sensory and transcendental ideas that Bill had interjected into his writings, in addition to the religious materials–primarily the Bible–which had provided the foundation for each of the three programs mentioned above. I have discussed the basic roots at some length in my title, *Turning Point: A History of Early A.A.'s Spiritual Roots and Successes*, and in studies of individual roots to be mentioned hereafter. To these must now be added the principles and program of the United Christian Endeavor Society to which Dr. Bob belonged as a youngster and whose ideas closely parallel the Akron pioneer program in most details. This likely additional source has been the subject of several of my recent writings (Dick B., *God and Alcoholism*; *When Early AAs Were Cured and Why*; *Cured: Proven Help for the Alcoholic and Addict;* and *The James Club and The Original A.A. Program's Absolute Essentials*). The Christian Endeavor source is also introduced in my article on Christian Endeavor posted at http://www.dickb.com/Christan_Endeavor.shtml and the sites of several others as well e.g. http://www.alchemyproject.org/articles . Furthermore, most of the Christian Endeavor root is now discussed at some length in my latest title, *The James Club*; but some much needed additional research and investigation are still current works in progress.

The Six Major Religious Roots I Have Previously Publicized

I have written many materials on what seemed to be the six major religious roots of A.A. I wrote the materials *seriatim* as I investigated and discovered the facts. And it is fair to say that Henrietta Seiberling was thoroughly conversant with each of these six sources and the literature that accompanied them. However, since I began my research over sixteen years ago, additional sources have surfaced or come to my attention; and these will be discussed at a later point below.

The Bible

Dr. Bob said quite plainly, and a good many times, that A.A.'s basic ideas came from their study and effort in the Bible. He emphasized the Book of James, Jesus's Sermon on the Mount, and 1 Corinthians 13 as "absolutely essential." All the basic ideas which the pioneers borrowed from the Bible were first discussed in detail in my title, *The Good Book and The Big Book: A.A.'s Roots in the Bible.* The basics were later amplified in *Turning Point*, then presented as a guide in *Why Early A.A. Succeeded* and in *Twelve Steps for You;* and then made the principal topic in my title *The James Club and The Original A.A. Program's Absolute Essentials*. Moreover several recent analyses of the biblical ideas the pioneers utilized from James, the Sermon, and Corinthians have been posted in my website articles. See http://www.dickb.com/index.shtml Many other sites have also published this data. [http://www.waterwagonsandiego.com/alcoholism_101.htm (accessed

7/15/04) and http://www.biblestudynotes.org/html/resources/resources.htm (accessed 7/15/04)].

Whether you start with Dr. Bob's explicit statements about A.A.'s Bible source, or turn to its other major roots (Quiet Time, Anne Smith's Journal, the life-changing program of the Oxford Group, the teachings of Rev. Sam Shoemaker, or the Christian literature early A.A. pioneers read), you meet the Bible head on. And my own interviews of Henrietta's children, their letters to me, and my examination of Henrietta's Bible (and the many notes inside of it) make clear her studies and familiarity with all these same A.A. Bible roots and sources.

Quiet Time

No believer familiar with the countless references in the Bible to seeking and receiving revelation from the Creator can ignore the Quiet Time practices of the A.A. pioneers. Everything about those practices was Biblical, and they were not in any way related to Eastern chants or bizarre meditation techniques. The pioneers observed Quiet Times in their homes, at the Smith home, and at their meetings. In so doing, they subscribed to the Bible basics involving a new birth, Bible study, prayer, seeking God's guidance, and use of devotionals. They sought God's guidance in their set-up meetings and in their regular meetings. Acceptance of Christ–having the indwelling spirit of Christ–was a must. Bible study was a must. Prayer and seeking guidance were musts. And the use of devotionals like *The Upper Room, The Runner's Bible, The Meaning of Prayer, Daily Strength for Daily Needs, Victorious Living,* and *My Utmost for His Highest* was among the most common of the "helpful books" they relied upon. Their use was regular fare. See my title, *Good Morning!: Quiet Time, Morning Watch, Meditation and Early A.A.*.

Further, there was scarcely a book–whether written by Rev. Sam Shoemaker, included in other Oxford Group literature, mentioned in Anne Smith's Journal, or directly addressing quiet time–that did not enthusiastically urge on its readers, including A.A. members, the regular practice of quiet time. And both Bill and Lois Wilson and Dr. Bob and Anne Smith read the recommended devotional books and observed the practice. Henrietta was no exception.

Even more interesting in our latest research was our discovery of the specific practices of United Christian Endeavor. One of the most important parts of their program was what was called Quiet Hour. There was even an honored membership called "Comrades of the Quiet Hour." The practices derived from the same sources (such as Dwight Moody, F. B. Meyer, and Henry B. Wright) that were drawn on in later years by Dr. Frank N. D. Buchman and Rev. Sam Shoemaker for Oxford Group Quiet Times. Thus, whether the Akron practices derived from United Christian Endeavor (as I believe they did) or from the Oxford Group (which they certainly did in New York), Quiet Hour or Quiet Time or The Morning Watch), they were a major part of the program's Bible foundations and ideas.

Anne Smith's Journal

As I have pointed out many times, the journal of the early ideas and program that was kept, read, and used for teaching by Dr. Bob's wife has just plain been ignored by A.A. itself and by historians who talk about its history. Strangely, this vital piece of history has been excluded from Dr. Bob's Home–the very home were A.A. began and where Anne and Dr. Bob lived. Yet Anne's writings in her journal began in 1933 and continued through 1939. The journal discussed and explained each one of the A.A. sources in one way or another. And it certainly dealt in detail with the A.A. Quiet Time practices. See my title, *Anne Smith's Journal, 1933-1939.* It is a reading must for anyone who desires or purports to be versed in A.A.'s spiritual program and practices.
It should have been (and as desired by Ray G., the archivist at Dr. Bob's Home) and hopefully will become a major part of our historical treasures in Akron. Thanks to the warm reception given to me by those in charge of the Seiberling Gate Lodge exhibits at Stan Hywet Hall and Gardens, this material will at least be known and seen at that historical landmark–now to be visited frequently by A.A. members and others at Founders Day observances in Akron.

I have found no evidence that Henrietta either read or listened to the contents of Anne's Journal. However, there is ample proof that Henrietta and Anne talked to each other frequently on the phone, visited each other, attended meetings together, and expressed themselves in much the same way when it came to the Bible, the Oxford Group, and the Christian literature of early A.A.

The Teachings of Rev. Samuel M. Shoemaker, Jr.

Sam Shoemaker's footprints are everywhere in A.A.–though he's virtually unknown today and seldom mentioned. In Akron, he was responsible for Russell Firestone's 1931 victory over alcohol. While Sam did not attend Akron's 1933 Oxford Group events, his numerous books, sermons, and articles were in wide circulation generally and certainly in all Oxford Group circles. His Calvary House in New York was the virtual headquarters for the Oxford Group in the 1930's. He kept in touch with Presbyterian pastor J. C. Wright in Akron as to progress being made in the alcoholism arena after his protege, Bill Wilson, stayed with the Smiths in the summer of 1935. Soon Shoemaker became a close friend of Bill Wilson's. Bill consulted with him during the period Wilson was writing the Big Book. Bill asked Sam to write the Twelve Steps (though Sam declined in favor of Bill). Shoemaker had led many of the Oxford Group meetings that Wilson attended, and he actually reviewed the Big Book manuscript before it was published. It seems quite clear that every one of the twelve steps bears Shoemaker marks–something Bill himself later acknowledged. See *The Language of the Heart: Bill W.'s Grapevine Articles*. NY: The AA Grapevine, Inc., 1988, pp. 296-300. (To the point where Wilson finally dubbed Rev. Sam Shoemaker a "co-founder" of A.A.

Shoemaker's influence in Akron and on Akron A.A. was far less direct. There is no strong evidence that either Bob, Anne, or Henrietta had much, if any, direct contact with him. Dr. Bob's son Smitty told me he had never heard of him and asked, "Who is he?" There is ample evidence, however, that Shoemaker's books were read by all the Akron pioneers and by other A.A. pioneers as well. Henrietta's children pointed out to me Henrietta's interest in Shoemaker's books. And, for additional, specific details on Shoemaker and A.A., see my titles, *New Light on Alcoholism: God, Sam Shoemaker, and A.A.* and *The Books Early AAs Read for Spiritual Growth*, 7th ed.

The Life-changing Program of the Oxford Group

Despite long-standing efforts by Bill Wilson, by various Roman Catholic clergy and writers, and even later by A.A. members and professionals to put a lot of distance between A.A. and the Oxford Group, the efforts didn't really succeed. Those destructive plans involved speculative assertions that tried to link to A.A. (In place of, or addition to its clear Oxford Group roots) and give supposed historical prominence to the Exercises of St. Ignatius, New England transcendentalism, "liberal"

Protestantism, New Thought Movement writers and writings, New Age idolatry, and even Swedenborgian thinking.

Yet, on the East Coast of the United States, every facet of A.A.'s history is nailed solidly to the Oxford Group, whether you speak about Frank Buchman, Sam Shoemaker, or the many Oxford Group activists like Rowland Hazard, Shepard Cornell, Cebra Graves, Ebby Thacher, Hanford Twitchell, Rev. Garrett Stearly, Victor Kitchen, Phillip Marshall Brown, Rev. Jack Smith, Rev. John Cuyler, Rev. Ray Purdy, Rev. Cleve Hicks, Rev. Howard Blake, or Rev. and Mrs. W. Irving Harris. These were people of many religious persuasions, Lutheran, Presbyterian, Dutch Reformed, Episcopalian, and Anglican. All are mentioned, one way or another, in the writings and diaries of Lois Wilson and Bill Wilson when speaking of their Oxford Group days. If not mentioned by those two, then in the personal journals of Rev. Sam Shoemaker, which I have seen and of which I have copies, that linked most of the names interchangeably with Wilson's.

To the extent Wilson could handle the material, he had been exposed to every feature of the Oxford Group program: (1) Belief in God and His plan. (2) Sin as the problem. (3) Surrender to God. (4) The Five C's of life-changing–Confidence, Confession Conviction, Conversion, and Continuance. (5) Jesus Christ as the Cure. (6) The Four Absolutes as the moral standards set by Jesus Christ as tests for truly Christian living–Absolute Honesty, Purity, Unselfishness, and Love. (7) Restitution. (8) Quiet Time and its requirements of accepting Christ, Bible study, prayer, guidance, journaling, checking, and use of devotionals. (9) A spiritual experience, witnessing, fellowship, and practicing Christian principles in one's life.

As we will show, the Oxford Group had less of an influence on the Akron program than most have assumed. First, the little group of Oxford Group people and alcoholics consisted of about 50-50 each. Their focus was on helping drunks. The pioneers called themselves a Christian Fellowship–not the Oxford Group. Their meetings were called "old fashioned prayer meetings"–more like revival meetings, according to Dr. Bob's son. The surrenders upstairs closely matched the healing ministry of the Book of James, rather than any Oxford Group practices. Akron mandated new birth through acceptance of Jesus Christ as Lord and Saviour. The Oxford Group did not–often speaking of a "Power" or "Higher Power,"seemingly unrelated to God's son, Jesus Christ. The frequent visits by most or all of the alcoholic squadron members to newcomer alcoholics who had been hospitalized during their first few days of sobriety was unique to Akron. And, because of its variations from any Oxford Group format, Oxford Group activist T. Henry Williams said the Akron group was more like a "clandestine lodge" of the Oxford Group. Ultimately, the Akron people withdrew from what Dr. Bob called the "shackles" of the Group although they acknowledged and expressed much appreciation for the altruistic roles played by T. Henry and Clarace Williams and their other brothers and sisters in the Group.

Henrietta's personal affiliation with the Oxford Group was solid. Congressman Seiberling emphatically told me: "My mother, I am sure, read all the Oxford Group books of the 1930's." And he named several of them. When I reviewed with him the twenty-eight Oxford Group principles which I had found to have influenced A.A., I asked him if he was familiar with them. He replied, "I would have to have been deaf not to hear them because my mother spoke of them all the time." And for the complete Oxford Group picture and full explanation of the twenty-eight principles, see my title, *The Oxford Group and Alcoholics Anonymous: A Design for Living That Works*.

The Christian Literature the Pioneers Read and Studied

One of the reasons so many A.A. histories have missed the mark of completeness and accuracy in reporting's A.A.'s start is that the historians seem never to have looked at, read, or appreciated the significance of the wide variety of Christian literature that the Akron pioneers read. One of the latest historical meanderings focuses on some 1940 list of 10 books the pioneers were supposed to have read, but there is no reference to the hundreds of books in Dr. Bob's library, Anne Smith's Journal, the Oxford Group itself, the thirty-book production line of Sam Shoemaker's books, or the extant collections of Henrietta Seiberling and of the venerable Clarence Snyder who got sober in 1938 and was sponsored by Dr. Bob.

Careful research has disclosed to the point of demonstration the innumerable books that Dr. Bob read and circulated among the early A As and their families (See Dick B., *Dr. Bob and His Library*, 3rd ed.). Many of these same books appeared on the reading lists and in the libraries of Henrietta Seiberling and old timer Clarence H. Snyder (See Dick B., *The Books Early AAs Read for Spiritual Growth*, 7th ed., and *That Amazing Grace: The Role of Clarence and Grace S. in A.A.*). To these lists must be added the books specifically recommended by Anne Smith in the journal she shared with the pioneers (See Dick B., *Anne Smith's Journal, 1933-1939, 3rd ed.*). Finally, there was an immense number of Oxford Group, Shoemaker, and meditation books in existence and being read and mentioned in early A.A. circles (See Dick B., *The Oxford Group and Alcoholics Anonymous*; *New Light on Alcoholism: God, Sam Shoemaker, and A.A.*; and *Good Morning!: Quiet Time, Morning Watch, Meditation, and Early A.A.*). The magnitude of these materials can be appreciated by reading my comprehensive bibliography, *Making Known the Biblical History and Roots of Early A.A. 3rd ed.*, which describes the 23,900 historical items I collected during my fifteen years of research. All these items impacted one way or another on the reading, studies, thinking, and discussions in pioneer A.A.

Early A.A. reading fell into many categories. These are a few: (1) The Bible; (2) Books on the life of Jesus Christ; (3) Books by and about the Oxford Group; (4) The books, writings, and sermons of Rev. Sam Shoemaker; (5) Popular books of that day by Harold Begbie, Brother Lawrence, Oswald Chambers, Glenn Clark, Lloyd Douglas, Henry Drummond, Harry Emerson Fosdick, Emmet Fox, Toyohiko Kagawa, E. Stanley Jones, and Leslie Weatherhead; (6) Many books on Christian healing, prayer, and meditation; (7) psychology; (8) spiritualism; (9) psychic matters; (10) the Emanuel Movement; (11) Christian classics by St. Augustine and Thomas a Kempis; (12) many on how to study the Bible; and (13) daily devotionals such as *The Upper Room*, *My Utmost for His Highest*, *Daily Strength for Daily Needs*, *The Runner's Bible*, *The Meaning of Prayer*, and *Victorious Living*.

And Henrietta Seiberling studied and taught from the contents of many of these as did Anne and Dr. Bob Smith and T. Henry Williams–a Baptist.

Other Literature--Less Mentioned, or Un-researched, Yet Significant

When I first began looking for and at the literature that early pioneers read or which influenced their ideas and program, I became so excited at the scope and importance of the foregoing six roots that I overlooked several other sources that were to require further research. Thanks to some diverse resources and suggestions, I learned that my quest for a comprehensive understanding of A.A.'s spiritual roots was far from complete.

Carl Jung and his titles

Some critics have expressed distaste for Jung's views. Others have disputed his connection and influence with A.A. Still others have asserted he was not a Christian. But, whether you like the Jung connection or not, one strongly supported view in A.A. is that Jung's advice to Rowland Hazard that Rowland needed a conversion was what really set the A.A. ball rolling. Wilson was prolific in his mention of Jung's role. Bill claimed it helped A.A. people to have conversions on a wholesale basis. Jung's book *Modern Man in Search of a Soul* was read by both Dr. Bob and Bill. Bill even inscribed and gave a copy to Dr. Bob. Therefore, whether the "spiritual experience," "religious experience," "spiritual awakening," and "conversion experience" talk in A.A. (and ultimately in Bill's Twelfth Step) can be attributed solely to Jung is something we still do not know. This because many Oxford Group writers, Rev. Sam Shoemaker, William James, and others also used these terms but insufficiently defined them and inadequately reported their origin.

William James and his titles

Called the father of American psychology, Professor William James of Harvard most assuredly had an impact, both direct and indirect, on A.A. Wilson claimed that his early reading of James's *Varieties of Religious Experience* validated Bill's own "hot flash" experience in Towns Hospital. Bill also claimed that his First Step idea of "deflation at depth" came from James's book. One A.A. historian (Ernest Kurtz) disputes this; but my own study of William James's frequent references to the "crisis of self-surrender" uncovered ample evidence that James was in fact talking about "deflation of self" and "deflation of the ego" as the turning point–the starting point–in any religious life. This is true whether Bill Wilson spotted that clear-cut point or not during his fuzzy days of early sobriety at Towns Hospital when he first read the James book. In fact, I don't know how any careful researcher could miss William James's deflation point. The "crisis of self-surrender" and the "turning point" language of William James was, in fact, picked up by Rev. Sam Shoemaker in his very first book, *Realizing Religion.* Sam quoted and discussed these terms frequently in his later books. They can certainly be found in Chapter Five of A.A.'s basic text.

William James is also one of several New Thought writers who seem to have given birth to the curious "higher power" idolatry that has now become embedded in 12-step literature and thinking. And it must be conceded that both Dr. Bob and Bill read James's *Varieties* book, whatever they may have borrowed from or accepted (if at all) of its contents.

The "New Thought" writings

I had a hard time with this one.

"New Thought" has been said to embrace Ralph Waldo Emerson and transcendentalism, Phineas P. Quimby, Mary Baker Eddy and Christian Science, Ralph Waldo Trine's *In Tune with the Infinite*, the Fillmores and Unity, Frank B. Robinson and Psychiana, Emanuel Movement leaders, Emmet Fox, Religious Science, Divine Science, and others. Inevitably, these kindred writings have, by their critics, all been frequently tossed into the "kingdom of the cults." And for a breezy discussion of them in that vein, see Richard R. Mathison, *Faiths, Cults and Sects of America*, 1960; see also Mel B., *New Wine*, pp. 101-125. The problem I have with labels is that they are usually plastered on people of one belief by people of another belief who disagree. So, for a time, "new thought" for me was just a label, and one in which I had no interest in terms of my own religious beliefs and faith.

Many Christians claim that New Thought leaders and New Thought adherents were not and are not Christians. There are those also within the New Thought fold who concede that "new thought" ideas are different from those of most Christian denominations. Discussing Unity, Divine Science, and Religious Science. New Thought proponent Mel B. said: "Although these organizations are outside mainstream Christianity, their literature has had considerable influence throughout American society" (Mel B., *New Wine,* p. 105), and Mel is probably right. In a scholarly study of religion and healing, Dr. Leslie D. Weatherhead devotes a good portion of his book to an examination and criticism of Christian Science (Weatherhead, *Psychology Religion and Healing*, 1951, pp. 151-196). And the following appear to support the indictment of New Thought groups as "non-Christian." Weatherhead says: "I am afraid no Christian could possibly accept Mrs. Eddy's theories" (p. 179). "Who is right? Mrs. Eddy in her affirmation that sin does not exist and that salvation consists in realising it, or the Fourth Evangelist [John] . . ." (p. 195); and "Where it is recognizable Christianity at all, it is Christianity without tears" (p. 196). In his cult book, Richard Mathison comments: "There are certain paradoxes which confuse the observer. . . . There is no baptism, and the Church rejects the Trinity, a personal God, the devil, atonement, the Resurrection, heaven and hell" (p. 68).

Such comments and others often lead other New Thought adherents to deny the common roots and relationship of Christian Science to New Thought. As to Unity and Christian Science, Mathison says: "Their cause was different in a number of respects. Unlike Christian Science they claimed that sickness and death were real, but added that both could be overcome by mind. . . . The denomination denies its earlier kinship with Christian Science, as do Mrs. Eddy's followers" (Mathison, *Faith Cults, and Sects, supra,* pp. 69-71). As to "New Thought" itself, Mathison says:

> "Today, New Thought is metaphysical, though in a strictly 'philosophical sense,' leaders say, distinct from orthodox Christianity in that it does not believe in the Trinity. Also, unlike Christian Science, it does not deny the reality of the material world. Rather, it declares, 'the physical world is Mind in Form'." (p. 75).

Of Frank Robinson and his Psychiana, Mathison says:

> "What were his wondrous lessons? They were essentially an adaptation of the old "Boston Craze" or New Thought movement. All had the common element of awakening in a pupil his own potential through the power of suggestion. They instructed the student with specific methods on how to better his life through introspective analysis. They kept him with a sense of expectancy and hope. In 1939, Dr. Robinson called on Westbrook Pegler, who had been lambasting him. 'I am not interested in saving souls,' he told the columnist, I want to raise the mental and spiritual sights of the people'." (pp. 109-110).

It appears that Bill's good friends, Rev. Sam Shoemaker and Rev. and Mrs. Irving Harris, were among those who didn't see New Thought adherents as Christians. Rev. W. Irving and Mrs. Julia Harris were named by Bill Wilson as major factors in A.A. development. They lived at Calvary House along with Shoemaker. Irving was Shoemaker's assistant minister, and Julia was in charge of the book stall there where Shoemaker and other Oxford Group literature was sold or distributed. And Julia said to me in an extended phone conversation with her at her home in New Jersey, with reference to New Thought writer Emmet Fox: "We were not sure he was a Christian."

Shoemaker wrote the following in his first significant book, which was copyrighted in 1921:

> There is a lot of palaverous optimism in these new cults, but one can find a terrific amount of unhappiness beneath it. One of the most ardent supporters of New Thought with whom I am acquainted, far superior to the rest of us in "knowledge of the Spirit" (whatever that deliciously vague and occult idea means), happens to be a most unhappy person, who has never made the most elementary adjustments for peace within his own walls. It is not that the cults are not emphasizing something important which orthodox religion has neglected, and that is just what all heresies come from; but the presentation is partial, lacks the solidarity and roundedness which we long for in our faith (Shoemaker, *Realizing Religion*, pp. 6-7).

Others have said with some frequency that the writings like those in Mary Baker Eddy's Christian Science (which both Bill W. and Dr. Bob read) were neither Christian nor science. Even more significant is Emmet Fox's own writing where he baldly claimed there is no doctrine of salvation in the Bible. Fox also claimed as myths certain biblical concepts such as sin and atonement (See Emmet Fox, *The Sermon on the Mount.* New York: Harper & Row, 1934, pp. 4-5, 7-8). Fox had his own way of interpreting Bible miracle accounts. Fox's thinking about the Pauline epistles shows Fox's own bizarre interpretation of Colossians 1:27.

The Apostle Paul, minister of the gospel to the Gentiles, refers to the "mystery" and then states that the facts were made known to the saints. He said that God had made known to them the glory of this mystery among the Gentiles which, Paul said, "is Christ in you, the hope of glory." Paul was making quite clear that the Gentiles too "should be fellow heirs, and of the same body, and partakers of his promise in Christ by the gospels" (Ephesians 3:6). And Paul was talking about those Gentiles who were born again of the spirit, saved, and had confessed Jesus as Lord and believed in their heart that God had raised him from the dead (John 3:16; Romans 10:9).

Fox must have been infatuated with his own "universalism"–the same universalism that Lois Wilson claimed had been adopted in A.A. because "all drunks were not Christians." Fox went a few steps further than Lois Wilson. He took the "Christ in you" language and proposed that *everyone* has Christ in him. Fox appeared to teach that "Christ in you" was free for the taking, that the death and resurrection and ascending of Jesus to the right hand of God was not merely the accomplishment for those who believed, but for anyone and everyone, if at all.

Reflecting this contention, New Thought advocate and A.A. old-timer Mel B. recently said to me he didn't think early A.A. people were John

3:16 Christians. Frankly, I don't know of any other kind, and there is nothing in the early A.A. surrenders to Christ that suggests otherwise. And note Colossians 1:26:

> Even the mystery which hath been hid from ages and from generations, but now is made manifest to his saints: To whom God would make known what is the riches of the glory of this mystery among the Gentiles; which is Christ in you, the hope of glory.

This meant: Christ in those who confessed with their mouth Jesus as Lord, believed in their heart that God raised Jesus from the dead, and thereby received the spirit of Christ (Romans 10:9). These, the Bible tells us, are those who became part of the body of Christ. Not just anyone, as Fox contends, but those who saw and heard the message in the Book of Acts that there is salvation in no other name than that of Jesus Christ of Nazareth (See chapters two and four of the Book of Acts).

Yet I've heard the New Thought stuff more than once in A.A. From my first grand-sponsor who has never read the Bible, is not a Christian, and yet recommends Fox's *The Sermon on the Mount* for reading by his sponsees. I've recently located quite a few references in New Thought writings to the odious (to me) "higher power" idolatry. I have read Sikorski's *A.A.'s God-parents*, which–without any documentation–bestowed the hallowed "godfather" title on Jung, Fox, and columnist Jack Alexander. Mel B. suggests: "There are some grounds for believing, too, that the term conscious contact, which appears in AA's Step Eleven, may have emerged from the lectures of Emmet Fox in New York City, which Bill and Lois attended with other AA members in the late 1930's (*New Wine*, p. 106). But these flimsy droppings-by-suggestion do not, in the absence of documentation, establish the depth of the supposed influence on A.A. But so much, then, for the continuing efforts to float Emmet Fox and New Thought ideas in today's A.A. Today, just about anything floats if it is repeated enough times in a meeting or quoted by an old timer.

For several years, I was turned off by all this unsubstantiated material! I couldn't believe from what I had researched and learned that New Thought had anything to do with early A.A. other than the fact that some of its literature was read. But I much respect Mel B. as a writer and historian; and we have become friends. His book *New Wine* contained extensive observations about alleged New Thought influence on A.A. These got my attention even though I was later to learn that Mel is himself a New Thought believer and very probably thinks he sees relationships between A.A. and New Thought that, at the very least, warrant more careful questioning and scrutiny as to their existence.

Then, however, I went to a "recovery" history conference in Rhode Island where a learned scholar took me to dinner and to a bookstore, all the while scolding me that I was overlooking the New Thought ideas in A.A.'s early years. He even bought me *The Portable Emerson.* He told me I needed to learn about this father of New Thought and Transcendentalism. He also suggested I needed to read the Big Book with greater focus on Emersonian ideas.

And, in the course of the next few years, I read Emerson, Mary Baker Eddy, Ralph Waldo Trine, William James, Emanuel writings, Thomas Troward books, Fox's books, and those by others in the New Thought stable. In fact, you too can take a peek at the dimensions of this group (Unity, Christian Science, Science of Mind, etc.) by looking up the New Thought movement sites on the internet. Note too that, although some assert that New Thought is Christian, they add that it was expanded to embrace other religions as well.

From all these comments and materials, I came eventually to see a real unity among Wilson's unusual Big Book references to "Fourth Dimension," "choosing your own conception of God," "Power greater than ourselves," "Higher Power," "Creative Intelligence," "Spirit of the Universe," "Realm of the Spirit," "God consciousness," "Great Reality," and "Infinite Power and Love." Such capitalized words and phrases strongly suggested to me that Wilson had, for sure, picked up a lingo, totally new and different from that he had gleaned from Sam Shoemaker and from the Smiths in Akron. As he penned the Big Book, he used language you didn't see or hear when you looked at Akron A.A. And you just can't square the New Thought stuff with what Bill heard and absorbed from the Bible in his early Akron days.

To be sure, Wilson liberally salted his Big Book with references to the Bible's God, Creator, Maker, Spirit, Father of Light, "Faith without works is dead," "love thy neighbor as thyself," "Spirit," "Thy will be done"–all undoubtedly reflective of Bill's association with the Smiths, Henrietta, and the Williams couple in Akron. As well as with the Episcopalian"Bible Christian" Rev. Sam Shoemaker and the "Bible-soaked" Oxford Group's Lutheran founder Dr. Frank Buchman.

Nonetheless, it seems inescapable that Wilson appropriated a new "spiritual" root and mixed it in with Akron's decidedly "old time"

Christian principles and practices. Or, at least Bill was strongly influenced by the words he heard in this new material. Bill added to his earlier vocabulary, and concocted in his A.A. thinking all this new stuff (that clearly now to me) smacked of New Thought, spiritualism, ESP, Emanuel Swedenborg, Rudolph Steiner, William James, plus Theosophical, and even the later-to-follow New Age dogma. This other-world transcendental stuff did not seem to come from Akron. It can't be squared with the "old fashioned revival meetings" that bystanders saw and described. Yet some of Dr. Bob's reading certainly did include these subjects. This presumably because Dr. Bob had a wide interest in current religious literature of the day. But the foregoing language of the "fourth dimension" world does not appear in any of the early Akron materials I have seen. It seems to have reared its head and to have gained historical prominence as Bill Wilson's secretary, Nell Wing (a Buddhist) started providing the names of books she claimed were popular in early A.A. (See Bill Pittman, *AA The Way It Began*).

You have to concede today that A.A. is *no longer* Christian. One of Bill Wilson's biographers opines:

> Wilson did not want to impose his views on others. However, the compromises he brokered about how to characterize the role of God in A.A.'s program for spiritual conversion clearly reflects his thinking on the subject. Over the next thirty-three years, Wilson's writing and speaking would be characterized by a continuing refusal to introduce Christian doctrine to AA (Francis Hartigan, *Bill W.: A Biographer of Alcoholics Anonymous Cofounder Bill Wilson*, NY: St. Martin's Press, 2000, p.124).

The problem for Hartigan is similar to the problem that other present-day historians and biographers have when they look at A.A. They just don't want to see the Bible or Jesus Christ or Yahweh the Creator that were ever-present in the minds and hearts of Akron pioneers. In fact, Dr. Bob's daughter, Sue Smith Windows, often said pointedly in her many talks to A.A. members, "There were *two* founders of A.A., you know." That, of course, is the point we have emphasized in sixteen years of research and twenty-six published titles.

It is a point that some of the new A.A. history writers have begun to discuss and tout. Wilson started out on one track—a track probably congruous with that of Dr. Bob—but he hopped on a new one once he was free of Akron influences. Thus in his recent biography of Dr. William D. Silkworth, Dale Mitchel points out:

> Several sources, including Norman Vincent Peale in his book *The Positive Power of Jesus Christ*, agree that it was Dr. Silkworth who used the term "The Great Physician" [referring to Jesus Christ as writers often called him] to explain the need in recovery for a relationship with Jesus Christ. If true [and Peale documents that it is], this reference to Jesus has all but been eliminated from Alcoholics Anonymous history. In the formation of AA, Wilson initially insisted on references to God and Jesus [just as did Dr. Bob and the Akron people], as well as the Great Physician. As the fellowship grew, however, other members persuaded Bill that a purely Christian format would alienate many, keeping potential members away from joining the group (Dale Mitchel, Silkworth: *The Little Doctor Who Loved Drunks*. Center City, MN: Hazelden, 2002, p.50).

Amen. And amen! How long it has taken for this simple set of facts to be acknowledged by prestigious A.A. history writers. Of course, Lois Wilson contended there had been an agreement to eliminate Christianity because, as she put it, all drunks were not Christians. But her allegation was never documented. Earlier, historian Ernest Kurtz had noted that there had been a total omission of Jesus. But neither person bothered to point out that it was Bill himself who had contended for the Great Physician and who had wanted the Jesus and God references to be reported and made in his Big Book.

Yes. There were two founders, you know. And, there were two A.A's, you know! In one of the typical biographical efforts to distance Wilson from the Oxford Group and Christianity, Francis Hartigan lets the cat out of the bag:

> Yet there is also much about the Oxford Group that is not carried over into AA. Alcoholics Anonymous is not a Christian Fellowship. There are no specifically Christian references in any of its literature (Hartigan, *Bill W.*, p. 65).

Amen. And Amen! Provided we are talking about the A.A. of today. But, wow! Where was Hartigan when they were passing around the Big Book! Has he ever read Bill's speeches? Has he ever read Bill's accounts of what went on in the summer of 1935 in Akron? Has he ever read James, the Sermon on the Mount, or 1 Corinthians 13? Did he have the slightest idea that most of the language in the Twelve Steps is that taken directly from "A First Century Christian Fellowship" called the Oxford Group! Has he ever seen what Dr. Bob and Bill talked about in public when they were on the stage together! Perhaps he knew these things but believed his readers would diminish in number if told the complete facts. And that seems to be where most historians stand: Don't tell the whole story or book sales will diminish or the "God-bitten" will be kept away from the fellowship. A nice thesis, but what about the truth? As Silkworth himself observed, it was Jesus Christ that made the difference. Yes. Jesus was crucified and buried. But present-day writers have forgotten about the resurrection, and about how pioneers relied on it.

Today, A.A. is not a Christian Fellowship.

Today, lots of its leaders write that it is not even "religious" though many courts have held otherwise in commonsense rulings.

Today, A.A.'s "trusted servants" seem to be duty-bound to eliminate mention of the Bible or Christian literature or Jesus Christ. But it is still there in the distant shadows. Just read the Co-founders biographical sketches and last talks that are printed in a pamphlet available at most meetings. Despite the historical truths, many of 12 Step groups and writings "ban" "religious" material from A.A. meetings. New thought idolatry has heavily impacted on, and gained ascendancy amidst the swirling "spirituality," "higher power," "universalism," "inclusive but not exclusive,"secular and self-made religious talk in today's treatment and 12 step programs.

I hold my nose when I observe these things, but extensive research and reading have persuaded me that psychic and extra-sensory thinking have rolled heavily into "recovery" ideas by the appending of new far-out religious thoughts to those stemming from early A.A. reliance on the power of Yahweh our Creator.

The writings of and about Dr. William Duncan Silkworth and Richard Peabody. I leave to the writings by others, particularly Dr. Norman Vincent Peale, and also to my own studies elsewhere the significance of Silkworth and Peabody. Silkworth, who unquestionably believed and said that Jesus Christ was the Great Physician who could cure alcoholism, was known in A.A. primarily for his singular role in A.A. as the person who wrote the Doctor's Opinion in the Big Book, who ministered to Bill Wilson in Towns Hospital, and who provided Bill with some important ideas about alcoholism and how to convey them. But the Silkworth views on Jesus Christ, on healing, on the "Great Physician" just lie a-moldering in the grave of discarded truths. See the excellent rendition of these facts by the Dale Mitchel *Silkworth* book just out.

Peabody is another story. He was an unsuccessful lay therapist who wrote *The Common Sense of Drinking–a* book owned by both Bob and Bill. Peabody's ideas and language filtered into Bill Wilson's Big Book. These included the idea that "once an alcoholic always an alcoholic" and the idea that there is no cure for alcoholism. Peabody died drunk and proved his point, but his language and ideas remain in the Big Book today. Mel B., in *New Wine*, has provided good material on Peabody. *Silkworth.net* is a website that provides good material on Dr. Silkworth.

I mention both the Silkworth and the Peabody resources in my own websites.

The Newly-Emerging Seventh Major A.A. Bible Root–Christian Endeavor

It was a long time before I spotted this one.

My former colleague, A.A. historian Richard K., and I were just getting our feet wet in researching it when Richard decided to pursue a different course. Others have now taken up the cause.

Dr. Bob had mentioned his excellent training in the Bible as a youngster. Somewhat sarcastically, he spoke of three or four church or prayer meetings each week plus Christian Endeavor that he was "more or less forced to attend." His scanty remarks about his early church life suggested to me an unearthed and important paradox when I compared them to what I later discovered to be his life-long church involvement and biblical studies.

What did Dr. Bob do in Christian Endeavor? What did Christian Endeavor do? What did Christian Endeavor do that was different from what the Oxford Group did? What did Christian Endeavor do that was like what the Akron pioneer program did? Did it differ in any respect? Why were these matters not researched or discussed when so much of Wilson's biographical material has been so widely covered both in and out of A.A?

The answers will come before long after current extensive research is complete and analyzed. Who knows? We may soon discover that T. Henry, Clarace, Henrietta, and Anne were all involved in Christian Endeavor. I've recently seen strong evidence that the early Akron program closely resembled the simple principles of the Salvation Army. And to roots of Endeavor and the Army extended to the literature early

AAs read. Moreover, United Christian Endeavor certainly reached into Congregational, Methodist, Baptist, and Episcopal denominations whose churches had the Akronites as members. We have already discovered Christian Endeavor's importance to Presidents William Howard Taft, Herbert Hoover, Dwight Eisenhower, Richard Nixon, and Ronald Reagan. We've also learned that the predecessor of A.A.'s friend Dr. Norman Vincent Peale (Dr. Poling) left his pulpit in New York to be replaced by Peale and to become president of World Christian Endeavor. Who else is in the picture?

In an extensive recent article, I introduced this new possible Christian Endeavor root of A.A. See http://www.dickb.com/Christian_Endeavor.shtml. I compare Christian Endeavor's literature, handbooks, confession of Christ, Bible study, prayer meetings, and Quiet Hour, plus its emphasis on "love and service" with those same features in the Akron fellowship. And I see a close resemblance. Those very features appear in both Christian Endeavor and in early Akron A.A.–in the surrenders, Bible study, prayer, Quiet Hour guidance, love, and service work of the original A.A. Christian fellowship in Akron. For openers, see my titles: *When Early AAs Were Cured and Why; Cured: Proven Help for Alcoholics and Addicts; Why Early A.A. Succeeded; God and Alcoholism;* and *Dr. Bob and His Library*, 3rd ed. See also my major discussion and documentation in my new title, *The James Club and The Original A.A. Program's Absolute Essentials.*

The "Parade of Horrors" Argument

Lawyers often use a "parade of horrors"in arguing their case against someone or something. They often do it when the facts are not supportive of their convictions. "If you do this," they say, "just consider the terrible things that will happen." "If you don't do this," they say, "even worse things will happen." So just shut all the doors, they say. "Shut your eyes, close your ears, and don't listen to others. Listen only to what we are telling you. Think of all the horrible consequences of letting in the light." Any story but ours "might hurt you, or produce horrible consequences" they say. It might even blind you and drive others away from you, they say. This is the same subtle approach taken by some well-intentioned A.A. members, historians, and biographers.

I've probably used that type of approach myself in trial courts and appellate briefs. But I'd hate to see it continue to flourish in the new A.A. censorship-scare mentality. So many committed A.A. members today are tossing aside the truth about pioneer A.A. They warn of the dangers of allowing anyone to write or distribute or discuss anything that has to do with the Bible, the Creator Yahweh, Jesus Christ, church, religion, or ill-defined "non-conference approved" literature.

As a temperature test, I recently asked an A.A. Trustee (who is a physician) about A.A. "Spirituality." I asked him for a definition, and I wish you could have heard the confused, theoretical babble he uttered in response. He—a trustee of our outfit!. Then I read a letter on A.A. General Services stationary, in which the writer purported, on behalf of A.A., to talk about A.A.'s views of a "Higher Power." And just who authorized that garbage, I wonder. If not A.A. itself, then she was out of line. If A.A., then A.A. has some historical study to do if it intends to convey accurate, impartial information from its World Headquarters in New York. The typical views of these two people at A.A.'s top "servant" level, however, do not reflect the A.A. of the late 1930's which documented a 75-to-93% success rate among medically-incurable alcoholics who really tried. The views exclude the truth and mindlessly ignore the widely surveyed, and ever-plummeting membership attendance and success rate in A.A. today. You yourself wouldn't purport to speak on A.A.'s behalf, whether as Trustee or General Services employee, but ignore A.A.'s own more recent survey results which report a static or declining membership and a success rate of about 1%. You wouldn't ignore the early religious picture and try to foist idolatry and "spirituality" on listeners if you were forthright about A.A.'s sources. Why expect any less from A.A. leaders and "trusted servants?"

One unrelenting proponent of today revisionist "not-god-ness" A.A. makes the following contribution to the parade of horrors:

> Less happily, there have also recently appeared people, who in pursuit of particular agendas tell A.A.'s story in ways that distort its history. Of particular concern are the Oxford Group enthusiasts who try to provide historical underpinning for what has become a movement to Christianize Alcoholics Anonymous by reinterpreting A.A.'s early history. Some of these zealots at times directly denigrate the contributions of Sister Ignatia and Father Dowling in their singe-minded, indeed narrow-minded, attempts to prove that A.A. came out of "Bible Christianity." It is unlikely that you will confront many of these people directly, because usually they do not have much contact with Catholic clergy. But they tell their versions, and some of the distortions and half-truths get spread around (Ernest Kurtz, *The Collected Ernie Kurtz*. WV: The Bishop of Books, 1999, p. 112).

Indeed they do great spread around, Ernie. What gets spread around is the truth about A.A.'s Bible roots; and that truth has nothing to do with the importance of the good Sister Ignatia or the status of the Jesuit Priest Father Dowling and his "spiritual sponsorship" of Bill Wilson. Recently, a Roman Catholic priest who holds a masters and doctor degrees endorsed my books and coined the word "lacuna" to describe the historical hole that people like the distinguished Ernie have dug. Poor Ernie! In fact, I say "God Bless you, Ernie." The foregoing vitriol has more than once been quoted by one or two of your friends as indicating your views of my work. But never directly by you yourself to my face or in correspondence, by email or phone, or otherwise. I'd suggest that the reader and Ernie himself take note that many today let our love and tolerance code go by the board in favor of distaste for religion, drunks, and Protestants. This very nonsense is what Wilson's Twelve Traditions tried to eliminate—controversy over politics and religion. Quite frankly, I don't have a problem with Jews, Protestants, Pentecostals, or Roman Catholics and their beliefs and interests in A.A. or their religious denomination. I have a lot of problems with those who don't want to hear about their experience, strength, and hope or about the experience, strength, and hope expressed by our Founders in Almighty God. In the foregoing quote, the author makes statements that are patently wrong and undocumented. And he makes them with uncontrolled emotion. Why not let the facts speak for themselves: Either there is invasion of A.A. by Oxford Group "enthusiasts" or there isn't. Frankly, I have attended thousands of meetings and have never encountered an Oxford Group enthusiast other than 100 year-old Jim Houck who is an Oxford Group member. Actually, the Oxford Group today–with its tiny membership, changed name, and non-Christian emphasis–is scarcely like the Oxford Group that Kurtz attacks. Actually, Oxford Group survivors like Houck are appalled at the Group's drift from God. I'm not an Oxford Group "enthusiast, and I don't know of many in A.A. except 100 year old Jim Houck who got sober before there was an A.A.

Another point: Either there is a group of storm-troopers involved in a blitzkrieg invasion of, and attempt to Christiantize A.A. (Let's label these mythical invaders Aggressive Facists Christianizing Alcoholics Anonymous). And they either exist, or they don't. Frankly, I find that the believers who are leaving A.A. for Alcoholics for Christ, Teen Challenge, Overcomers, Overcomers Outreach, Alcoholics Victorious, and Celebrate Recovery are leaving in droves because there no longer is observable Christianity in A.A. or its meetings. Wake up, Dr. Kurtz! There's no invasion into A.A. There's a Dunkirk where Christians are scrambling for boats leaving it. Take a look at the hundreds of self-help, atheist, humanist, Christian, Roman Catholic, and other non-A.A. groups in the recovery scene today. Then you decide whether you need to climb in a hole, shiver and shake, and hide from the alleged invading Christian A.A. hordes. I don't know of such a group of invaders, and after personally seeing the A.A. hate letters directed at the late Clarence Snyder, I don't see any threatening "movement" in A.A. that is coming from the 352 or more Christian denominations, if they ever recently agreed on anything–including A.A. (See Mitchell K., *How It Worked*, pp. 214-229, and Dick B. *That Amazing Grace*, pp. 17-19, 61-63, 86-87, 108-112).

As to the paranoid claim that "people" are denigrating Catholic clergy (naming Sister Ignatia and Father Ed Dowling as the supposed victims), I hear this nonsense every time I make a history address in Akron. There are lots of good people in Akron—good AAs, good Roman Catholics, and good members attending meetings there. Yet if I come to Akron to speak, I start getting anonymous phone calls and letters telling me that I have left the good Sister and the good Father out of A.A. history! They usually hang up before I ask if they have read my books to find out.

How could I? There is a fine book by Mary Darrah out, and being accorded an exclusive position at Dr. Bob's Home. It's *Sister Ignatia; Angel of Alcoholics Anonymous*. I usually cite Darrah's book in my numerous bibliographies and mention the Ignatia era and story wherever appropriate. And when I've gone to Founders Day addresses in Akron, there have been only three blown up pictures on the stage–Bill W., Dr. Bob, and Sister Ignatia. People are run around during Founders Day with purple buttons that announce they visited the Sister Ignatia Ward at St. Thomas Hospital. As to these folks, is there: Denigration? Abandonment? No I'd say it's adulation, and it's quite appropriate if you set that diamond properly in an appropriate ring setting..

Similar thing for Father Ed Dowling. Kurtz pushed, and finally got published, a book about Father Dowling and Bill Wilson. It's written by a Roman Catholic Jesuit Priest, Father Bob Fitzgerald. It's called the *Soul of Sponsorship*. It covers the Wilson-Dowling correspondence. It's a great book. And Dowling was given center stage in many of Wilson's writings–particularly the inclusion in Bill's *A.A. Comes of Age* of Dowling's address at the A.A. Convention in St. Louis.

Both Darrah's book and Fitzgerald's book were, according to what each of the authors told me, financed largely by a Jesuit organization. Was this funding blocked? Were these books banned? Did someone attempt to suppress their circulation in A.A.? Denigration? Abandonment? No, I'd say deserved adulation. And outside funding! Again, just put the gems in the right setting.

I do.

This belated effort to inflate the importance of Sister Ignatia and Father Dowling as against the deriding of the Oxford Group, the Bible-thumpers, and the Christian storm-troopers is absurd. It's what lawyers call a "straw man" argument. If you have no case, you set up a "straw man" to knock over in order to divert attention from your own weak argument. And the alleged denigration of Roman Catholic authors is pure nonsense. There are far more Roman Catholics in A.A. and in America than there are Christians in any other religious denomination. They're hardly ignored!

What's everyone afraid of? Someone just wrote me that too much history may drive our Roman Catholic and Jewish friends away and leave A.A. as a Christian Protestant Fellowship. But that is just blind absurdity. No way! We are long past that point. Anyone–just anyone–can frequent the rooms of A.A. today. Roman Catholics predominate. And, in case A.A. scaremongers have forgotten, Roman Catholics, Jews, and Protestants all read their particular versions of the "same" Scripture manuscripts. Most believe in the same God--our heavenly Father, Yahweh, the Creator of the heavens and the earth. And most should be able to remember a favorite World War II picture of four chaplains singing "Praise the Lord, and pass the ammunition."

I remember that song and the picture of four chaplains of different religious faiths. They weren't denigrating each other. They were engaged in the common cause–victory in World War II and survival in battle. They worked together, but they didn't check out religious qualifications. And that should be the situation in A.A. today. In fact, it is! Only the writers do the name-calling.

Why stir up religious animosity. I recently led an A.A. retreat meeting at a Roman Catholic monastery. A Roman Catholic Brother opened and closed the retreat. I read from a Roman Catholic approved Bible, and I wasn't stoned. I was there by invitation. I addressed the group on A.A. history for hours and hours. Nobody was denigrated–certainly not the good brother, or the monastery, or the Roman Catholic faithful who came to hear about A.A. They were there to hear about A.A. history, not about someone's religious prejudices or silent resentments..

So let's open the doors, stop fanning the flames of division, banish the fears, and let people know the whole–I said whole–A.A. history. Let people of all beliefs or no beliefs decide for *themselves* in A.A. *itself* exactly how they will approach the problem of curing alcoholism. It's the divisions and revisions that drive people away—not the truth about A.A. and its rich history. I don't personally care about the faith of the four chaplains passing the ammunition. And I don't personally care who steps up to the firing line in A.A. if that person really wants to help drunks. He or she can be a Methodist, Buddhist, Presbyterian, Jesuit, Hindu, atheist, or rabbi. Recently a writer disputed my well-evidenced statement that all are welcome in A.A. He cited the flak he receives as an atheist. But that's part of A.A.'s completely open door policy today. Atheists sit side by side with Christians and with the "bleeding deacons." A few even throw stones at each other now and then. In that venue, A.A. newcomers *still need* all the help they can get from the outreaching A.A. members–whether those volunteers are atheist, Baptist, or Hottentot. They don't need the fueling of the fires like that which takes place in Ireland over religion and destroys people.

Fie on those who spread fear. Fear of religion. Fear of church. Fear of Christianity. Fear of mentioning God or His name. Fear of unrestricted reading, disclosure, and discourse. Fear of truth in today's A.A. meetings and among some who write about A.A.

My belief is that some of today's writers have become so far removed from the wet drunk and alcoholic—certainly from sponsorship of these newcomers--that they really don't know the need or how it was met and can be met. The current parade of nonsense should become a parade that nobody cares to see or support. It's an illusory parade of illusory horrors, and it's not getting anyone cured! Drunks ministering to drunks with God's help can and does!

3

Henrietta's Special Role as a Non-Alcoholic Woman Who Helped Found A.A.

This segment will be short, but it will help to highlight the importance of Henrietta Seiberling to the founding and development of Alcoholics Anonymous in Akron. And let's look at exactly what she brought to the scene.

- Henrietta was not an alcoholic.
- She was a highly intelligent woman, a Vassar grad, a reader of many books, and a student of the Bible.
- She believed in God, was a Christian, and attended a Christian church.
- She was beset with personal and marital problems and had found relief with God and His word.
- She was thoroughly conversant with the Oxford Group, its principles, literature, and practices.
- She belonged to the same church as, and was a good friend of, Anne and Dr. Bob Smith.
- She knew of Anne's faith, her bewilderment over Bob's drinking, and her devotion to Bob.
- She took a very personal interest in trying to help Anne and to bring Bob to sobriety.
- She was the catalyst who brought Anne Smith to the Oxford Group meetings in 1933.

- She was the catalyst who rather quickly got Dr. Bob interested in meetings and the Oxford Group itself.

- She read many of the same books, pamphlets, and articles that Dr. Bob read.

- She organized the meeting at which Dr. Bob was persuaded to confess his plight.

- She informed Dr. Bob that God had revealed to her that Bob must not touch one drop of liquor—a precept that certainly was not an Oxford Group idea.

- She specifically invited Bob and the tiny Oxford Group squad to pray for Dr. Bob's success in overcoming drinking.

- She fielded the call of Bill Wilson for a drunk to work with.

- She immediately recognized the Oxford Group principle of "passing it on."

- She perceived Wilson's need for someone to help. She understood Wilson's persistence in trying to reach her after many calls. And she appreciated the relevance of Bill's Oxford Group roots and their similarity to those with which Dr. Bob was familiar.

- She thought to herself, "This is Manna from Heaven" and told Bill she had just the man for him.

- Next day, Bob's son brought him to Henrietta's; and Henrietta introduced Bill and Bob at her Gate Lodge home where they had their six hour meeting.

- She put Bill up at the Portage Country Club to keep him on deck.

- She helped plan, attended, and often led the set-up meetings and regular Wednesday night Oxford Group meetings before and after Bill joined the Akron group.

- She kept in close touch with Anne, worked with Bob and Anne to help drunks, and counseled many of the drunks herself.

- She was commended by Bill for the success that she, Bob, and Anne were having with the Akron program during the many months Bill was absent in New York..

- She emphasized and observed Bible study, prayer, quiet time, and personal work with others.

- She remained committed to the A.A. society for as long as she lived.

- She and Bill Wilson were in touch with each other long after Dr. Bob's death.

- She had compassion when Bill and Bob both needed understanding and compassion.

- She was a teacher when A.A. needed teachers.

- She was a believer when A.A. needed believers.

- She knew her Bible when A.A. was searching the Bible for answers and stressing its study.

- She knew Oxford Group, Shoemaker, and Christian writings and shared their contents with the pioneers.

- She became a self-appointed critic of Bill Wilson's later drift from A.A.'s religious roots and reliance on God; and she plainly stated her views to Bill and others.

- Her life was peppered with concern for, and work with, other people.

- Her life and gravestone monument were underlined with: "Let go, and let God."

4

Akron's Oxford Group Encounters

We have more to say about Henrietta Seiberling, the Oxford Group, Akron, and Alcoholics Anonymous. The account must really begin several years before A.A.'s founding on June 10, 1935. Most of it is told at greater length in my titles, *The Akron Genesis of Alcoholics Anonymous* and *The Oxford Group and Alcoholics Anonymous.* The details are very well supplemented in: James D. Newton's *Uncommon Friends,* T. Willard Hunter's *Uncommon Friends' Uncommon Friends* and his title *It Started Right There,* as well as A.A.'s "Conference Approved" *DR. BOB and the Good Oldtimers.*

The Special Role of James Draper Newton

How strange it seems that a man who never had a drink would set in motion the greatest alcoholism recovery society of all time–a fellowship that was specifically tailored to bring about the cure of alcoholism. The man was James Draper Newton who was to become a good friend and a tremendous supporter of my research into the relationship of the Oxford Group to Alcoholics Anonymous. As he lived into his nineties, Jim had had active personal contact with Oxford Group founder Dr. Frank N. D. Buchman; with Rev. Samuel M. Shoemaker, Jr. (whom Bill Wilson called a "co-founder" of A.A.); and with one of the earliest Oxford Group woman activists and writers–Newton's wife to be–Eleanor Napier Forde.

Newton's personal Oxford Group friendships cris-crossed with many people so important to the development of Alcoholics Anonymous in Akron and on the East Coast of the United States. These people included Harvey Firestone, Sr., Russell (Bud) Firestone, Leonard Firestone, and Dr. Walter Tunks of Akron. They included Shoemaker, Rowland Hazard, F. Shepard Cornell, Rev. W. Irving and Julia Harris, Charles Clapp, Jr., Victor Kitchen, Kenaston Twitchell, Hanford Twitchell, Olive Jones, L. Parks Shipley, Rev. Garrett Stearly, T. Willard Hunter, Rev. Ray Purdy, Rev.Cleve Hicks, Rev. Howard Blake, Professor Philip Marshall Brown, George Vondermuhll, Jr., T. Henry Williams, and a host of others on the Oxford Group businessmen's team to which Bill Wilson belonged on the

East Coast. And they included many of the Oxford Group team members in Great Britain–Buchman's biographer Garth Lean, Michael Hutchinson, Kenneth Belden, Loudon Hamilton, Bunny Austin, Sydney Cook, Dr. Morris Martin (Buchman's secretary), and others.

Now to a condensed version of Jim's Akron impact.

Jim was born in Philadelphia in 1905. In 1923, he became a Belber luggage salesman and wandered into an Oxford Group meeting while in Massachusetts. He soon began his life-long Oxford Group activism. But the real estate boom in Florida was calling. Jim went there and, with the help of his father, established a real estate development known as Edison Park. It was situated between the homes of the famous Thomas Alva Edison and Henry Ford. Before long, Jim counted himself a good friend of both Edison and Ford and, not long thereafter, with their frequent visitor from Florida's East Coast–Harvey Firestone, Sr. Young Newton was capably handling the famous Edison birthday parties; and Harvey Firestone was so impressed with what he saw and with Newton himself that he asked Jim to come to Akron and become "Secretary to the President" of Firestone Tire and Rubber Company–later grooming Newton for the presidency itself. Newton did hold some important Firestone positions, but he later opted to devote his time to the Oxford Group and his Florida activities. But these later decisions did not hinder Newton's impact on Akron

During his employment by the Firestone company, Jim and two of the younger Firestones (Harvey, Jr. and Russell) became his good friends. Jim, however, was soon to discover that Russell had a monstrous drinking problem. Jim was so desirous of helping his friend Russell ("Bud") that he actually accompanied Russell to a treatment facility. He also worked with Russell to help him through the application of Oxford Group life-changing principles. But more was required. Newton persuaded Russell to take a train trip to a Denver conference of Episcopal Bishops. Russell was drinking a fifth of liquor a day and was in bad shape. Rev. Sam Shoemaker was in attendance at the conference. And, on the return train ride to Akron, Rev. Sam Shoemaker took Russell into a train compartment where Russell gave his life to Christ.

Russell returned to Akron cured–to the amazement of family, friends, and his physician (who called it a miracle). After which, Russell Firestone and Jim Newton began traveling and witnessing ("sharing for witness" is what the Oxford Group called it) to what God had done for them through changing their lives in the Oxford Group.

The change in Russell was so dramatic that it prompted Harvey Sr., Newton, and Dr. Walter Tunks (Rector of St. Paul's Episcopal Church where Harvey Firestone, Sr. and his family attended) to set up some huge testimonial events. These took place all over Akron during a period of about ten days in early 1933. Dr. Frank Buchman himself came to Akron with some 30 Oxford leaders. Protestant church pulpits were opened to Buchman, his team, the Firestones, Newton, and others. Akron society turned out in bushels. The newspapers covered every detail–specifically detailing Oxford Group principles such as surrendering one's life to God, Bible study, prayer, Quiet Time, the acceptance of Christ, and changed lives. And foremost among those witnessing was Russell Firestone–who testified to his own life change, his overcoming alcoholism, and his new interest in Christianity, the Bible, prayer, the Oxford Group, and his wife and family.

Unquestionably, Jim Newton was instrumental in getting Russell Firestone to turn to God and the Oxford Group for victory of alcohol. He then traveled widely with Russell once Russell got sober in 1931. Jim had much to do with the Oxford Group's virtual "invasion" of Akron in 1933. He himself spoke in one of the testimonials. Jim's wife-to-be (Eleanor Napier Forde) had already published her well-known booklet, *The Guidance of God*, whose contents somehow found their way into the journal kept by Dr. Bob's wife Anne Smith. Anne specifically mentioned Eleanor Forde's talks. And Jim's own connection with Akron continued as he headed the building fund campaign for the new St. Paul's Church in 1936.

I want to mention also that Jim Newton and Oxford Group veteran Willard Hunter furnished me with an immense number of names, addresses, phone numbers, introductions, leads, information, books, articles, and reminiscences about the Oxford Group. These were vital to my writing of *The Oxford Group and Alcoholics Anonymous*, *New Light on Alcoholism* (about Rev. Sam Shoemaker), *The Akron Genesis of Alcoholics Anonymous*, and *Good Morning* (about quiet time, morning watch, and meditation). The Newtons (both of them) and Hunter supported my research and publishing financially. And all ultimately turned over to me their respective libraries of Oxford Group books, thereby greatly enlarging my personal resource materials. I consulted and visited with each quite frequently to get answers to questions within their respective realms of memory and expertise.

Henrietta Jumps at the Opportunities

Akron's widely publicized "Firestone" testimonials and meetings in 1933 did not escape the notice of Henrietta Buckler Seiberling.

Henrietta had problems, her own problems. She also knew that Anne Smith, the wife of Dr. Robert H. Smith, was distraught over her husband's alcoholism. And she could not have escaped reading and hearing that Russell Firestone, the drunk, was in the news, the pulpits, and the podium telling how God had healed him of his problems, including alcohol. So Henrietta hustled Anne Smith and two other ladies to a huge meeting at the Mayflower Hotel; and they investigated for themselves.

Ere long, they were attending Oxford Group meetings; and soon after, they persuaded Dr. Bob to start coming to the meetings. Dr. Bob loved the people and their talk. He read all the Oxford Group literature he could get his hands on. He followed suggestions about Bible study, prayer, quiet time, and church attendance. He "refreshed" his memory of the Bible, pointing out that he had received "excellent training" in that as a youngster. He read the Bible from cover to cover three times. His library attests to the fact that he read a great deal of non-Oxford Group Christian literature as well–books like Henry Drummond's *The Greatest Thing in the World*; Oswald Chambers's *My Utmost for His Highest* and *Studies in the Sermon on the Mount;* the Methodist quarterly *Upper Room;* many books by E. Stanley Jones (including *The Christ of the Mount*); Glenn Clark, Emmet Fox (and his *The Sermon on the Mount*); Harry Emerson Fosdick (and his *The Meaning of Prayer*); and also Nora Smith Holm's *The Runner's Bible.*

But Dr. Bob didn't get sober. Why? He simply wasn't ready to quit drinking.

And, despite what some erring historians have suggested, the fault did not lie with God, Jesus Christ, the Bible, the church, Bob's prayers, his Christian fellowship, his religious studies, or the Oxford Group. The fault lay right at Dr. Bob's feet. Some might say that he still had a "disease" of which he needed to be cured. Many in A.A. today might say he had not "recovered."

But Dr. Bob didn't want to quit drinking! Not yet! And, without fulfilling that prerequisite, no real alcoholic stays sober for very long and in fact may never quit. And Dr. Bob confided that very weakness to Henrietta Seiberling. He wondered why he couldn't quit, and Henrietta assured him he just hadn't found the answer yet.

But Dr. Bob was to learn, if he did not already know, from one of his favorite books *in* the Bible–the Book of James–*the problem was temptation* (James 1:12-16). The solution required patience and asking wisdom of God without wavering (James 1:2-8). It meant submitting to God (James 4:7); resisting the devil and his devilish "wisdom" (James 3:13-17; 4:7); and believing without any doubt that God will make a way to escape so that you will be able to bear the temptation (1 Corinthians 10:13). For--says James in the Good Book--the devil will flee from you if you do submit to God, keep his word, and resist the devil (James 4:7). As Rev. Sam Shoemaker often commented: (1) "The devil comes back along familiar paths"–tempting with liquor in the case of the alcoholic. (2) Many of us need a kind of "divine derrick," said Shoemaker–to lift us out of the tempting mire; and James 4:10 promises that God will do the lifting if we make the humble submission:

> Humble yourselves in the sight of the Lord, and he shall lift you up (James 4:10)

And there are useful parallels in the Gospel of Luke. First, in Luke 8:11-15, Jesus explained the parable of the sower and the need to resist temptation; the need to keep God' word with an honest and good heart; and the fruit that comes from obedience:

> Now the parable is this: The seed is the word of God. Those by the way side are they that hear; then cometh the devil, and taketh away the word out of their hearts, lest they should believe and be saved. They on the rock are they which, when they hear, receive the word with joy; and these have no root, which for a while believe, and in time of temptation fall away. And that which fell among thorns are they that have heard, go forth, and are choked with cares and riches and pleasures of this life, and bring no fruit to perfection. But that on good ground are they, which in an honest and good heart, keep it and bring forth fruit with patience (Luke 8:11-15)

Note the sequence: First, there is the word of God which is to be heard and obeyed. Then the devil appears and steals the word from the hearts. The listeners heard the word and, for a time believed it, but succumbed to temptation. They had heard, but yielded to anxieties and pleasures, instead of keeping the word. And let's turn again to the A.A. favorite (the Book of James) which declared in James 1:21-22:

> Wherefore lay apart all filthiness and superfluity of naughtiness, and receive with meekness the engrafted word which is able to save your souls. But be ye doers of the word, and not hearers only, deceiving your own selves (James 1:21-22)

God's word plainly tells the reader that excessive drinking and drunkenness are wrong, are sin. (See Galatians 5:21–drunkenness; 1 Peter 4:3–excess of wine; 1 Corinthians 5:11-a drunkard; 1 Corinthians 6:10–drunkards; Romans 13:13–drunkenness). Long before the New Testament, Proverbs 23:29-35–in a section well-known to some A.A. students–gave a graphic picture of the drink, the drunk, the disaster, and the inexplicable determination to do it again:

> Who hath woe? Who hath sorrow? Who hath contentions? who hath babbling? who hath wounds without cause? Who hath redness of the eyes? They that tarry long at the wine . . . At last it biteth like a serpent, and stingeth like an adder. Thine eyes shall behold strange women, and thine heart shall utter perverse things. . . . I will seek it yet again.

Been there? Done that? As it is with so many ex-drunkards, so it was with me. Just go listen to an A.A. drunkalog and get it from the horse's mouth. The A.A. drunkalogs recount the same type of behavior thousands of years after God laid it out so plainly for all to see. Yet Bible students like Henrietta and Dr. Bob and the pioneers were able to see the Bible's solution–submitting to God, resisting the devil, and receiving the promise that the devil would flee. Note Luke's account of how Jesus resisted the devil, being tempted by him for forty days. Jesus resisted the temptations, turned to, quoted, and kept God's word; and devil fled–for a time. Luke 4:1-13:

> And Jesus being full of the Holy Ghost returned from Jordan, and was led by the Spirit into the wilderness. Being forty days tempted of the devil. And in those days he did eat nothing: and when they were ended, he afterward hungered. And the devil said unto him, If thou be the Son of God, command this stone that it be made bread. And Jesus answered him, saying, It is written that man shall not live by bread alone, but by every word of God. And the devil taking him up into an high mountain shewed unto him all the kingdoms of the world in a moment of time. And the devil said unto him, All this power will I give thee and the glory of them: for that is delivered unto me, and to whomsoever I will I give it. If thou therefore wilt worship me, all shall be thine. And Jesus answered and said unto him, Get thee behind me, Satan: for it is written, Thou shalt worship the Lord thy God, and him

only shalt thou serve. And he brought him to Jerusalem, and set him on a pinacle of the temple, and said unto him, If thou be the Son of God, cast thyself down from hence: For it is written, He shall give his angels charge over thee to keep thee: And in their hands they shall bear thee up, lest at any time thou dash thy foot against a stone. And Jesus answering said unto him, It is said, Thou shalt not tempt the Lord thy God. And when the devil had ended all the temptations, he departed from him for a season.

Henrietta Seiberling didn't miss a beat when it came to applying the Biblical principles just discussed. She sought to help her dear friends, the Smiths, and through the vehicle of their little Oxford Group meeting at the home of T. Henry Williams in Akron. She called a special meeting, said she meant business, and told the adherents there would be no "pussyfooting" about the steps to be taken. She asked that each come prepared to share "something costly"–consistent with the Oxford Group's method of "sharing for confession." She then sought wisdom from God and received revelation that "Dr. Bob should not touch one drop." This she told to Dr. Bob.

Her statement seems axiomatic in A.A. today. However, A.A.'s disease theory of allergy and obsession was not known to Henrietta and probably not to Dr. Bob either. So, believed Henrietta, the Creator was telling her plainly that the solution for Dr. Bob was total and complete abstinence.

That was the starting place–the warning revelation that Henrietta received from the Creator. *But Bob himself had to quit*. He himself had to resist temptation. He himself had to submit to God to be lifted up and out of what he later called the terrible curse of alcoholism.

Henrietta's meeting was convened. Dr. Bob came. Participants shared something "costly." And Dr. Bob cautiously joined in. He shared that he was a "secret drinker"–the "secrecy" notion being an illusion not uncommon for drunks. But, consistent with Oxford Grouper expectations, it was his own open admission that brought his problem to the fore, into the open and out for all to see and help. Whereupon Henrietta asked Bob if he would like to pray. Bob said, "Yes." The group, including Bob, dropped to their knees on the carpet of T. Henry's home, and prayed.

But Bob continued to drink. What about that? Was Henrietta's meeting in vain? Were the prayers ineffective? Had God let Bob down? The answers flow easily for a believer.

Consider what soon happened. Out of the blue, just a few short weeks later, the "way to escape"–the answer to the prayers–manifested itself in a most unusual way. The answer took the form of the unexpected and unusual appearance in Akron of a novice Oxford Group member from New York–an alcoholic Oxford Grouper at that. A drunk who had met financial misfortune in Akron, and had considered drinking as his way out. But that man (Bill Wilson) remembered the Oxford Group principle that he must give away what he had to someone else in order to "keep" it himself. In this instance, it was his sobriety that Wilson needed to share in order that he might "keep" it. At least that was the Oxford Group view. Henrietta knew her Bible: "freely ye have received, freely give" said Jesus in Matthew 10:8. She knew her Oxford Group materials: "Pass it on," Dr. Frank Buchman had written. "You have to give Christianity away to keep it," wrote Rev. Sam Shoemaker. There must be "sharing for witness," said a host of Oxford Group writings. Plainly this applied to Henrietta herself, and she must have known it. Even more clearly, these axioms enabled her to understand why this persistent Oxford Group newcomer, Bill Wilson, had gone to such lengths to work with another drunk.

Bill had sobriety, albeit tenuous. And just as his friend Ebby Thacher, only two months sober, had met with him, Bill knew that this was the Oxford Group way. If he wanted to stay sober, he believed, the Oxford Group people had taught him that he going to have to share his experience with another. This was Wilson's situation. He was discouraged over a business disaster, wanted to drink, had renounced drinking, and believed he could prevent another spree—**resist temptation**--by seeking out another drunk to help. Bill told Henrietta he was a "rum hound from New York." He told her he was a "member of the Oxford Group." He said he needed to find another drunk with whom to talk–someone with whom he could share his experience, strength, and hope. Just as Ebby Thacher had shared with him, scarcely more than six months before.

Henrietta arranged with Anne Smith for Bob to come to the Seiberling Gate Lodge (Henrietta's home). But the visit had to wait until the next day because Bob was drunk and unable to come. The next day Dr. Bob's son drove him to Henrietta's home to meet with Bill. Keeping his cards close to his vest, Bob had stipulated that he would only give "this bird 15 minutes. Tops." But the meeting lasted some six hours.

At the conclusion, Bill was proud as a peacock. He thought he had given Bob a powerhouse message about alcohol, the Oxford Group, and religious whatever. But Bob had an entirely different opinion of the lengthy meeting. He perceived and stated that Bill knew what he was talking about–that Bill spoke his language. As to alcohol, the Oxford Group, and religion? "No," said Bob in effect. He said he had heard it all before. But he was struck with Bill's honesty about his drinking and Bill's sincerity about the importance of "service" to others. And the latter was a concept which had not previously hit Bob as important in overcoming drinking.

How today does an alcoholic finally recognize his problem and admit he is licked? In A.A. at least, he hears from another the same bizarre and self-destructive behavior he himself has appropriated. How does he learn the solution? Surely not by just "going to meetings." Bob Smith knew full well that the solution had to come with God's help through prayer; and he had sought that at Henrietta' behest. What is the solution? Bob had heard it all long before there was an Oxford Group and long before he had met Bill. The basic idea in the solution was love and service: Love of God and one neighbor's love for another. Service to God and another just as you would want that love and service for yourself. Abiding by the so-called "golden rule" that Jesus had taught in his sermon on the mount (which verse can be found in Matthew 7:12). What else would help? Giving it away to keep it, just as Bill Wilson was doing. Just as the Oxford Group taught. And just as the Bible itself had made so clear about the ministry of reconciliation (See Mark 16:15: "Go ye into all the world, and preach the gospel to every creature;" Acts 1:8: "But ye shall receive power, after that the Holy Ghost is come upon you: and ye shall be witnesses unto me both in Jerusalem, and in all Judaea, and in Samaria, and unto the uttermost part of the earth;" 2 Corinthians 5:18: "And all things are of God who hath reconciled us to himself by Jesus Christ, and hath given to us the ministry of reconciliation").

And don't think for a moment that these Biblical principles learned in his youth at North Congregational Church and in Christian Endeavor did not come leaping back into Dr. Bob's remembrance.

The Bible and his "excellent training" as a youngster had taught Dr. Bob that there had to be belief in God; acceptance of Christ; the learning of God's commandments; obeying them; growing in understanding through prayer and study; seeking God's guidance; fellowshipping with like-minded believers, and witnessing. Though Bob's condition was shaky and sickly, the foregoing beliefs were the spiritual backdrop with which Bill Wilson was working.

Shoemaker had written many times that, to overcome *spiritual misery,* you need to seek a *spiritual solution.* That solution, said he in his very first significant book, was: "What you want is simply a vital religious experience. You need to find God. You need Jesus Christ" (Shoemaker, *Realizing Religion,* 1921, p. 9). These were things that had been hammered into Bob's mind by his church, by Christian Endeavor, and by his Bible. He didn't learn them from Bill Wilson. He knew them from the Bible. He believed God's word. And it all began to come together. This was the fullness of the answer to Henrietta's, Bob's, and the little group's prayers on the carpet of the home of T. Henry and Clarace Williams.

And it took the wobbly service of a former conservative atheist, who had never cracked a Bible, and never belonged to a church, to catalyze the whole thing. This real picture of the Akron miracle has never been presented before to the Oxford Group people, or to present-day A.A. members, or to those concerned with "treatment." The total solution meant commitment to abstinence. It takes God and belief in the power of God. It takes coming to God through His son Jesus Christ. It takes the seeking of God. It takes obedience to God. It means establishing a relationship and fellowship with God and His son. It takes resistance to sin and temptation. And it takes fellowship and witnessing. All these principles represented the fullness of the things Dr. Bob had heard before. They added up to abstinence if and when Dr. Bob decided to quit drinking

Henrietta put Bill up at the Portage Country Club, and then Bill moved in with the Smiths for three months in the summer of 1935. The things that happened in Dr. Bob's home that summer were certainly not of an Oxford Group flavor. There were late night discussions of the Bible. There were meetings by Bill with Anne and Henrietta. There was daily Bible reading by Anne to Bill and Bob. There was daily prayer and quiet time. The focus of the study and efforts came to be, primarily: (1) the Book of James–their favorite, said Bill; (2) the Sermon on the Mount–containing the underlying philosophy of A.A., said both Bill and Bob; and (3) 1 Corinthians 13–whose ingredients as to the meaning, character, and importance love were strongly urged by Bob..

With these beginning discussions and experiences under their belt, Bill and Bob set out to find drunks to help. They soon found Bill Dotson (A.A. Number Three) who was an alcoholic lawyer in bad shape. They put him in the hospital, told him their stories, brought about his turn to God for help, and saw him walk from the hospital "a free man." This

Dotson was a man whom, as both he and Wilson later said, the "Lord" had cured." See *Alcoholics Anonymous*, 4th ed., p. 191.

Wilson said this deliverance experience of Dotson's marked the founding of the first A.A. *group.* The first group had miraculously been founded in Akron only a matter of days after Bob's last drink–an event (Dr. Bob's last drink), which became the acknowledged date of the A.A. fellowship's own "founding."

Meetings of the little band of Oxford Group people, alcoholics, and their families continued at the T. Henry Williams home for several years. Gradually, there were as many alcoholics as Oxford Group people in attendance. Later still, the alcoholics began meeting separately in the same home. And we'll discuss the program they were evolving for alcoholism's cure. They developed it primarily through their Bible study and effort and the effective instructions of Dr. Bob, Anne, Henrietta, and T. Henry Williams.

5

The Unique Christian Fellowship Program of the Pioneers

Distinguishing Akron's Program from Bill's Later Twelve Steps

You will never understand the Akron program unless you look at the real picture, the whole picture, the complete picture, of the origins, founding, principles and practices of the first years of pioneer A.A.. Even those apologists for Bill Wilson, who ignore the specifics on the Akron program, seem reluctantly to concede the differences:

> Because the Twelve Steps have long been the treatment model embraced by nearly all substance-abuse treatment programs, it is hard to imagine that they could have been produced amid swirls of controversy. . . . When the project got under way, there seemed to be nearly as many programs of recovery as there were alcoholics who had recovered. . . . Getting agreement on the book itself was even harder (Hartigan, *Bill W.*, p. 114).

Hartigan's book is no more enlightening about the differences than any of the other contemporary histories. But it calls to mind again Dr. Bob's emphatic statement that he did not write the Twelve Steps and, in fact, had nothing to do with the writing of them.

Another writer observed:

> Although the breadth of A.A.'s varieties is a new phenomenon, the reality of diversity within Alcoholics Anonymous is not merely recent. A.A.'s differences were one reason why it developed in so decentralized a fashion. Early researchers were aware of that, but they fell into the easy (and enduring) trap of researching what was available - studying those A.A.s who welcomed their research. Influenced also by the secularization hypothesis shared by most sociologists of the era, they tended to overlook the Akron birthplace of A.A. and its more Oxford Group-oriented offspring, concentrating their attention on New

York A.A. and its derivatives (Ernest Kurtz, *The Collected Ernie Kurtz*, p. 4).

The Wilson Experiences

The first part of the A.A. picture had to do with New York. The New York story goes as follows: that Rowland Hazard treated for alcoholism with Dr. Carl Jung, went back to drinking, returned to Jung for an answer, and was told that his plight was hopeless unless he had a conversion. Jung recommended Rowland seek a religious association. Rowland became involved with the Oxford Group and became thoroughly familiar with its literature, principles, and practices. Rowland was cured. Then he and two other Oxford Group friends sought ought Ebby Thacher, an alcoholic who was about to be institutionalized for alcoholism. The judge turned Ebby over to Rowland's care. Rowland taught Ebby the Oxford Group precepts and placed Ebby at Calvary Rescue Mission which was run by Sam Shoemaker's Episcopal Church in New York. There Ebby made a decision for Christ. He quit drinking. He sought out his alcoholic friend Bill Wilson, and told Bill of his own cure. Bill then went to Calvary Rescue Mission seeking what Ebby had. Bill was drunk, but made his own decision for Christ at an altar call. Though drinking, he soon proclaimed he had been "born again." He also wrote, "I've got religion"—the same claim that Ebby had made to Bill. Bill checked in to Towns Hospital one more time, talked to Ebby some more about the Oxford Group program, surrendered to God "as Bill understood God," and had his "hot flash" experience which he believed to be his finding of God. It could have been an hallucination. But, whatever that experience amounted to, it brought an end to Bill's drinking. Bill set out to help other drunks, but had no success whatever.

The reason seems fairly obvious to me. Bill was a fervent messenger, but he had no real message. Bill had been a self-proclaimed "conservative atheist." He married a non-Christian Swedenborgian woman. He had never read the Bible. He had never belonged to a church. His secretary told me that he had never read much of things like the Oxford Group and Shoemaker literature then or in later years. And with six or less months of sobriety, he was hardly capable of expounding the Oxford Group or Bible ideas that were later incorporated into his own Big Book manuscript and the Twelve Steps.

The Akron Experiences

The picture in Akron was totally different. Dr. Bob's whole early family life had centered around church–the North Congregational Church in New Hampshire. Also in the burgeoning youth movement known as the Christian Endeavor Society which had a group in his church. And perhaps even in the St. Johnsbury Academy he attended. At the church and Christian Endeavor activities, Bob was soaked in prayer meetings, Bible study, Quiet Hours, Christian fellowship, confessions of Christ, and Christian love and service. And despite the recently concocted stories about Bob's not being a Christian, he himself never forgot the soaking–especially in his later years when he so badly needed help and wanted to help others by utilizing the training he had received. Bob continued his Christian church affiliations. He took his kids to Christian Sunday Schools. When he joined the Oxford Group, he dived back into the Bible, read it three times, and devoured Christian and Oxford Group literature of the day. He attended both Episcopalian and Presbyterian churches, in sequence, for the rest of his life. Once he achieved sobriety that sprang from his association with Bill Wilson, he gave the Bible, Christianity, and Christian fellowship full bore.

Bob and Bill talked Bible, Bible, Bible. They listened to Bible, Bible, Bible. And they developed a special interest in the Book of James, Jesus's Sermon on the Mount, and 1 Corinthians 13. These three Bible segments were to form the basis for Akron's program and success. And we have pointed out their elements in several different writings, *The Good Book and The Big Book: A.A.'s Roots in the Bible*; *The Akron Genesis of Alcoholics Anonymous*; *Why Early A.A. Succeeded*; *When Early AAs Were Cured and Why*; *Twelve Steps for You; The James Club and the Original A.A. Program's Absolute Essentials*; and two articles on A.A.'s roots in the three Bible segments. http://www.dickb.com/AAsJamesClub.shtml; and http://www.dickb.com/AAbasicideas.shtml

The heart and significance of these fundamental early A.A. touchstones of recovery still remain a virtual unknown to most A.A. members today.

The need to contrast Oxford Group experiences in Akron with the New York Experiences

Unlike the Oxford Group itself–the Oxford Group in which Wilson had cut his teeth–Akron's "alcoholic squad" was focused on helping drunks. It insisted on abstinence–which the Oxford Group didn't. It insisted on early hospitalization–which was not a part of Oxford Group work. It required confession of Christ–again not an Oxford Group prerequisite. It stressed Bible study and prayer–which were really less important in the Oxford Group than "life-changing" work. It conducted "old fashioned prayer meetings"–which was a moniker never applied to Oxford Group meetings or house parties. It held almost continuous fellowship meetings and called itself a Christian Fellowship–not the Oxford Group's "A First Century Christian Fellowship" or "Moral Re-Armament." Its adherents carried the message of cure by conducting daily visits to newcomers in the hospital.

Two Oxford Group ideas did, however, achieve major prominence in Akron–adherence to the Four Absolutes (from the book *Principles of Jesus* by Robert Speer) and the elimination of sin from one's life (which was an Oxford Group focus but most assuredly the focus of the Bible as well, and there with far greater insistence, intensity and detail).

What the Pioneers Learned and Did

Finding the Drunk

Their first prerequisite was finding a real, "seemingly hopeless, "medically incurable" drunk. Henrietta was the first to aid in the quest by rooting Bob out of his "secret drinking" hole and praying for the solution that turned up with Bill's visit. Bill's own searches in the hospitals, missions, and meetings in the New York area provided guidance as to where and how.

The Usual Hospitalization

Next, Dr. Bob would meet with the newcomer drunk and his family to get the lay of the land. Most of the time, the alcoholic was then hospitalized. Only a Bible was allowed in his room as reading matter. Dr. Bob visited him every day and often talked to him for hours. Then other pioneers would visit, share their experience, and tell the newcomer that help was on the way. At the end of five to seven days, Dr. Bob would visit. He'd ask if the drunk believed in God; and, if he did, the patient was asked to get down on his knees and pray with Dr. Bob. This was the man's "first" surrender.

Home Fellowships

Next, many of the drunks were taken from the hospital into the Smith home. Later into the homes of others such as Wally G. and his wife, Tom Lucas and his wife, Clarence Snyder and his wife, and others. In a sense, these were the first real A.A. half-way houses. Wherever they were housed–at their own home or in other homes–the drunks would congregate at the Smith home at the crack of dawn to hear Anne Smith lead them in prayer, Bible study, seeking guidance, and discussing the items she shared from her journal. During the day, there were frequent fellowships, phone calls, visits from Henrietta, visits with Bob and Anne, as well as individual Bible study, reading, and prayer.

"Regular" Meetings

Mondays saw a set up meeting where, with God's guidance, a leader and topic were selected for the Wednesday meeting. The "regular" meeting on Wednesday was an Oxford Group meeting of sorts. But Oxford Group activist T. Henry Williams appropriately characterized it as a "clandestine lodge of the Oxford Group." Others described it as an "old fashioned prayer meeting." For its format was that of the Christian Endeavor of Dr. Bob's youth. It opened with prayer. Next, there was invariably reading from the Bible. Next group prayers, followed by a brief quiet time for guidance. There would be a discussion of some Bible topic or other matter applicable to their new lives. Sometimes the topic would be a Bible topic and sometimes a topic drawn from one of the devotionals like *The Upper Room.* The discussion would often be led by Henrietta, Dr. Bob, or T. Henry. Later, in the program's development, Anne Smith would share from the Bible or her journal for the discussion.

The "Real" Surrenders

At that point, new members were taken upstairs to T. Henry's bedroom where two or three would pray over and with him after the manner of James 5:16. He was led to accept Christ, to ask that alcohol be taken out of his life, and then to declare that he would live by the principles of the Four Absolutes. It is undisputed that, at these "real surrenders," as they were often called, the newcomer accepted Christ as his Lord and Saviour, became born again of the spirit of God, and emerged as one of God's kids.

The Afterglow

Downstairs again. Dr. Bob would recruit visitors for the hospitalized newcomers. The meeting closed with the Lord's Prayer and was followed by socializing. There was Christian and other Oxford Group literature on the table in T. Henry's furnace room; and it was taken or swapped by members. There were no steps. There no Big Book. There were no drunkalogs. There appeared to be no formal observance of Oxford Group procedures like confession, conviction, and restitution. There is evidence that, at a later point, Dr. Bob would meet with a newcomer, review his sins and shortcomings, and pray with him to have them taken away. And always, there was individual Bible reading, reading of literature, prayer, seeking of guidance, and use of daily devotionals like *The Upper Room* and *Victorious Living*. None of the devotionals was an Oxford Group book or pamphlet.

It was all just that simple. Finding a drunk. Hospitalizing the drunk. Sharing with him that there was hope and victory available at his own option. Confirming his belief in God and surrender to Christ. Enveloping him in a fellowship where he was taught Bible and Christian principles, prayed, and provided counseling from non-alcoholic "teachers" like T. Henry, Henrietta, and Anne Smith. Giving him all the support and tools and the power of God to enable him to resist temptation.

Emphasizing Three Special Parts of the Good Book

The early A.A. newcomer learned the principles of love and service from the "absolutely essential" three Bible segments we cover below.

The Book of James. He could find in the Book of James the need for patience, the availability of God's guidance, the life and death requirement that temptation be avoided, that God was the source of good things and that sins were devilish in origin, that faith in God must be accompanied by works, that loving and serving others were paramount principles, that the commandments of God–all of them–were to be obeyed, that fervent and effectual prayer produced results, and that he could be forgiven and healed by the Lord when asking for such in prayer. Also by the prayer of others for him.

The Sermon on the Mount (Matthew 5-7). He could find in the Sermon on the Mount the "Beatitudes" which Anne Smith taught were Christian virtues to be cultivated. He learned that he was to eschew anger, to reconcile with his brother, and to make restitution where needed. He was taught that Jesus called even for "love of enemies" and prayer for those who persecute. He learned the Lord's Prayer. He learned that God was his sufficiency and that he was not to be anxious for food, shelter, and clothing if he sought first the kingdom of God. He learned to look for his own faults before criticizing another's. He learned the Golden Rule. And he learned that the kingdom of God was for those who "do the will of the Father who is in heaven."

1 Corinthians 13. From 1 Corinthians 13, he learned the principles of love–nine of them–as Henry Drummond had discussed them in *The Greatest Thing in the World,* which was strongly recommended by Dr. Bob and widely read..

Repetition. Repetition. Repetition. These three Bible segments–James, the Sermon, and 1 Corinthians 13–were the absolutely essential elements. These provided the basic ideas, ideas which Dr. Bob called "foundational" for the Akron successes and later even to portions of the Big Book Steps. And the newcomer had help, lots of it. Henrietta, Anne, Bob, and Mr. and Mrs. Williams were all highly intelligent, well-educated *teachers.* They knew their Bible. They knew their Oxford Group. They knew their literature. And they practiced what they preached. Yes preached! Moreover, the newcomer was specifically urged to study for himself, to read the books that Dr. Bob circulated, and to use the devotionals that were given to, or made available to him. The newcomer had teachers. He had text books. The first "text-book" was "God's Big Book," as Dr. Bob's son used to refer to the Bible.

Akron's Christian Recovery Program As Described by Frank Amos in His Reports

As can be seen from the foregoing, there were no "Steps." There were no "drunkalogs." There were not even daily meetings as such. There was no basic text except the Bible itself. Nor was there even emphasis on the twenty-eight Oxford Group principles that were to impact on the ultimate A.A. program in Bill's Big Book (For details on the twenty-eight Oxford Group ideas, see my title, *The Oxford Group and Alcoholics Anonymous*).

Instead, there was insistence on avoiding temptation to achieve and maintain total abstinence.

DR. BOB and the Good Oldtimers reports:

> Remembering his own disastrous trip to Atlantic City and Bill's experiment with keeping liquor on the sideboard to prove it was no longer a temptation, Dr. Bob advocated that members stay in dry places whenever possible. "You don't ask the Lord not to lead you into temptation, then turn around and walk right into it," he said (p. 281).

Dr. Bob and Anne were great readers of the Bible, particularly Psalms, Proverbs, and the other parts we have mentioned. The following segments of James, Proverbs, and the "sermon on the mount", as well as Peter, were most certainly before their eyes to teach about temptation, the disaster of yielding to it, and God's ability and willingness to help:

> Blessed is the man that endureth temptation. . . (James 1:12).
>
> But every man is tempted when he is drawn away of his own lust, and enticed (James 1:14).
>
> Do not err my beloved brethren (James 1:16).
>
> Hell and destruction are never full; so the eyes of man are never satisfied (Proverbs 27:20).
>
> After this manner therefore pray ye: Our Father which art in heaven. Hallowed by thy name. . . .And lead us not into temptation, but deliver us from evil: For thine is the kingdom, and the power, and the glory, forever. Amen (Matthew 6:9, 13).
>
> The Lord knoweth how to deliver the godly out of temptations. . . (2 Peter 2:9).
>
> For if after they have escaped the pollutions of the world through the knowledge of the Lord and Saviour Jesus Christ, they are again entangled therein, and overcome, the latter end is worse with them than the beginning (2 Peter 2:20).
>
> Ye lust, and have not: ye kill, and desire to have, and cannot obtain: yet fight and war, yet ye have not, because ye ask not. Ye ask, and receive not, because ye ask amiss, that ye may consume it upon your lusts. . . . But he giveth more grace. Wherefore he saith, God resisteth the proud, but giveth grace unto the humble. Submit yourselves therefore to God. Resist the devil, and he will flee from you. . . . Draw nigh to God, and he will draw nigh to you. . . Humble yourselves in the sight of the Lord, and he shall lift you up (James 4: 2-3, 6-8, 10).

Once the duty to resist temptation and abstain were made clear in the original program, there was the further requirement of submitting to God and receiving the power of the Holy Sprit through accepting Christ. There were the teachings in the Bible and their Christian literature, about God, Jesus Christ, the gift of the Holy Spirit, prayer, guidance, thanksgiving, forgiveness, deliverance, and healing. There was the assurance that if they adhered to the principles of Corinthians, followed the rules in the Sermon, and relied on God for forgiveness, guidance, and healing as mapped out in James, they would do well. And all three of the major Bible segments laid out the vital necessity for love of, and service to, others–something that Akron did with astonishing success and surprising simplicity.

The Bible gave accurate and specific descriptions of the sins that constituted transgressions against God's commandments. And Dr. Bob got down to cases with each pigeon's sins. Earl T. of Chicago described his "moral inventory":

> Recalling the afternoon he spent with Dr. Bob in his office, Earl said, "He very carefully helped me through my moral inventory, suggesting many, many bad personality traits and character defects. When this was finished, he asked me if I would like to have these defects removed. Without much thought, I said, 'Yes, I would.' And then he asked me to get down on my knees at the desk with him, and we both prayed audibly to have these defects of character removed" (*DR. BOB and the Good Oldtimers*, p. 179).

Detours from the Truth

When people ask about the early A.A. program, they are often diverted by someone's mention of a supposed "six steps." But these varying, working ideas really did not exist either as "steps" nor did they have identical content. This seems clear from the fact that they were not mentioned in the biography of Dr. Bob and were, even though Bill later referred to them as "six" word-of-mouth steps, described by Bill in different and quite varying forms. He so stated and said, "Though subject to considerable variation, it boiled down into a pretty consistent procedure which comprised six steps" (and for a view of several of Bill's "variations," see Dick B., *The Akron Genesis of Alcoholics Anonymous*, pp. 256-257).

Then there's the curious content of a supposed "six" steps taken by Dr. Bob with Earl T. as described in one of the Big Book's personal stories.

But the very language of the numbered "steps"–joined in company with still other procedures that were taken–seem to me to be the product of Bill Wilson's editing, rather than a description of what Dr. Bob actually said and did with Earl T. In fact, other recognizable portions of the non-existent twelve steps are also set forth–suggesting Bill's confusion over what actually occurred (*Alcoholics Anonymous*, 3rd ed., p. 292).

Another problem arises from the fact that, for a description of the program, people are usually pointed toward the Big Book and Twelve Steps, which were written *after* the Akron program was developed and the cures were achieved. And the Big Book program (which Bill fashioned on his own with little comment from Dr. Bob and the Akronites) was far different from the original Akron program. As old timer Bob E. observed, "Henrietta [Seiberling] didn't like the book" (*DR. BOB, supra*, p. 217). A.A.'s own biography of Dr. Bob reported, "One problem was that some members wanted no part of the book". . . [Dorothy S.M. remembered] "For a time, we thought the whole Akron group might break up over the book" (*DR. BOB*, *supra,* p. 153).

Today, with the seeming intent of having them steer clear of the Bible and the early Akron Christian Fellowship, people are sometimes directed into the 1940's where–while Bill languished in deep depression–different groups developed different interpretations, different principles, and different practices. The Big Book was certainly the basic text, but the interpretations were fashioned by new people. In this later period (which one writer has urged as "back to basics"), the original Akron Christian program was not involved. Moreover, Dr. Bob himself was not a participant either guiding or in helping those various interpretive efforts except to the extent he had taught "pigeons" from Akron who went to work in areas like Cleveland, Detroit, Chicago, and Houston.

Dr. Bob's own efforts in the 1940's were centered on Akron Number One–the King School Group and on working in concert with Sister Ignatia helping some 5,000 drunks without charge, largely at St. Thomas Hospital. (See Darrah, *Sister Ignatia*). Furthermore, history reveals today that Dr. Bob continued to work until his death with his pigeons using the elements of the original Akron program, and the hospitalizations at City Hospital and at St. Thomas Hospital were said to be "basic training" for A.A. (See *DR. BOB and the Good Oldtimers,* pp.185-199).

The Cures in the Original Program

When Bill and Bob counted noses in Akron in 1938 to evaluate the success of the original program, they found that forty pioneers–"a hard core of very grim, last-gasp cases had by then been sober a couple of years," Bill said. "All told, we figured that upwards of 40 alcoholics were staying bone dry." (*DR. BOB, supra*, p. 123). This very clear statement has been carefully examined and reported in Richard K., *Early A.A.-Separating Fact from Fiction: How Revisionists Have Led Our History Astray.* (MA: Golden Text Publishing Company, 2003). Richard K. makes the strong point that there has been blatant, later re-editing of the records of the first forty, as to who they were, and as to the cures they achieved. Those early alcoholics were claiming positively that they were *cured.* (See Richard K., *So You Think Drunks Can't Be Cured*, MA: Golden Text Publishing Company, 2003; *New Freedom: Reclaiming Alcoholics Anonymous*, 2005).

They knew they had the elements of a successful program. Bill went to New York and to Rockefeller for money. Rockefeller sent his agent Frank Amos to Akron to investigate the facts. And Amos returned two highly enthusiastic reports to Rockefeller. Some of the details are given in *DR. BOB and the Good Oldtimers,* pp. 128-36; and the seven points of the program, as published by A.A. in *DR. BOB*, at page 131, were these:

The "Program"

Abstinence

"1. An alcoholic must realize that he is an alcoholic, incurable from a medical viewpoint, and that he must never again drink anything with alcohol in it.

Surrender to God

"2. He must surrender himself absolutely to God, realizing that in himself there is no hope.

Absolute Elimination of Sins from His Life

"3. Not only must he want to stop drinking permanently, he must remove from his life other sins such as hatred, adultery, and others which frequently accompany alcoholism. Unless he will do this absolutely, Smith and his associates refuse to work with him.

Morning Devotion and Quiet Time (with prayerful devotions, Bible study, and religious reading) **a Must**

"4. He must have devotions every morning–a 'quiet time' of prayer and some reading from the Bible and other religious literature. Unless this is faithfully followed, there is a grave danger of backsliding.

Helping Other Alcoholics a Must

"5. He must be willing to help other alcoholics get straightened out. This throws up a protective barrier and strengthens his own willpower and convictions.

Frequent Social and Religious Fellowship with Other "Reformed" Alcoholics

"6. It is important, but not vital, that he meet frequently with other reformed alcoholics and form both a social and a religious comradeship.

At Least, Weekly Attendance at Some Religious Service

"7. Important, but not vital, that he attend some religious service at least once weekly."

It's Time for Honesty about That Real, "Original" Program

It's time for alcoholics and the world to **revisit and know** the facts about the "original" A. A. program that was founded in Akron on June 10, 1935. Not the "original 12 Step program" that is being so characterized today. But the Akron Number One program with the astonishing success rates that ranged from 75% to 93% among real alcoholics who tried. The one that was developed in Akron primarily between 1935 and 1938. The one that was so simply and carefully reported to John D. Rockefeller, Jr. by A.A.'s trustee-to-be Frank Amos.

What the Original Program wasn't. It was not:

The Oxford Group program.

A "step" program of the Oxford Group–which had no steps.

A "six step" program of the Oxford Group–which had no steps.

The "word-of-mouth" six step program which Wilson described in various ways.

The "Twelve Steps" and Big Book–which were neither begun nor completed until 1938 and were not published until the Spring of 1939.

The Exercises of St. Ignatius, a version of Wesleyan ideas, or a pot pouri of eclectic religious ideas to sort out and master.

The so-called "original" 12 Step program recently fashioned and now being so publicized by an AA and his colleague, who is still an Oxford Group activist.

What the Original Program was. It was:

Bible-based: A program whose basic ideas arose out of Bible study and effort.

Focused primarily on three Bible segments: The Book of James, Jesus's Sermon on the Mount (Matthew 5-7), and 1 Corinthians 13.

First Century Christianity in action: A program that resembled the acts of First Century Christians as described in the Book of Acts–(1) meeting in homes; (2) calling for repentance and recognition of Jesus Christ as Lord; (3) preaching that God raised Jesus Christ from the dead; (4) relying upon the power of God as made available on Pentecost to those who believe; (5) praying; (6) studying God's word; (7) receiving revelation from God; and (8) ministering to unbelievers who wanted to receive the gift of the Holy Sprit and become children of the living Creator.

Developed by alcoholics and compassionate Oxford Groupers in Akron: Fashioned by a tiny group of alcoholics and non-alcoholic Oxford Group members–Dr. Bob Smith, Anne Smith, Henrietta Seiberling, T. Henry Williams, Clarace Williams, and Bill Wilson.

Completed in substance in the summer of 1935 and tested in the Akron crucible through 1938: Through study of James, the Sermon, and 1 Corinthians 13 which began the moment Bill moved into the Smith home in the summer of 1935–with Anne's reading to Bill and Bob from the Bible each day, late night discussions, the "spiritual infusion" by Anne and Henrietta of which Bill wrote, and prayerful consideration of the essentials. The rest–miraculous cure–was achieved almost immediately as exemplified by the manner and fact of the "cure" of A.A. Number Three (Bill Dotson) by the "Lord." See *Alcoholics Anonymous*, 4th ed., p. 191.

Closely paralleling Christian Endeavor Society practices: In a self-proclaimed Christian Fellowship whose actual beliefs and practices closely resembled those of the Christian Endeavor Society in which Dr. Bob had participated extensively as a youngster in his church. Simple Christian principles–confession of Christ, Bible study, old fashioned prayer meetings, Quiet Hour, reading of religious literature, fellowship and bringing others to a decision for Christ, "love and service." See my extensive discussion posted on my website: http://www.dickb.com/Christian_Endeavor.shtml. and the material in my new title, *The James Club*.

6

The Exit of the Oxford Group: Observations about A.A.'s Connection with the Oxford Group

First, the Oxford Group/A.A. connections on the East Coast that characterized the East Coast beginnings of A.A. were entirely different from those which were under way in Akron, Ohio.

The Carl Jung Story

Though now being disputed, histories have heretofore posited that the Oxford Group chain in the Eastern United States was linked to A.A. as follows: (1) Rowland Hazard treated with Dr. Carl Jung to overcome alcoholism. (2) Having failed with Rowland, Jung advised that only a conversion could help Hazard's chronic alcoholism. (3) Hazard linked up with the Oxford Group, was possibly converted, and practiced its life-changing principles. (4) The resultant victory message of hope was carried by Rowland and two others to Bill's alcoholic friend Ebby Thacher of Albany. (5) Ebby Thacher "got religion" in the Oxford Group and firmed it with a decision for Christ at Shoemaker's Calvary Rescue Mission in New York. (6) Ebby carried the victory message to his old friend Bill Wilson, telling Wilson that God had done for him what he could not do for himself. (7) Wilson went to Calvary Rescue Mission "looking" to "get" what Ebby had "gotten." Bill made a decision for Christ at the Rescue Mission altar; wrote that he been "born again" for sure, checked in to Towns Hospital; further reviewed Oxford Group ideas with Ebby; and then humbly asked God for help. (8) Wilson had in Towns Hospital what he came to believe was a "spiritual experience." (9) He never drank again. (10) Wilson, though unsuccessful in his efforts, sought to carry an Oxford Group message to drunks at Towns Hospital, at the Rescue Mission, and at Oxford Group meetings. (11) He met Dr. Bob in Akron at the behest of Henrietta Seiberling, and a wholly different approach began.

What A.A.'s East Coast Oxford Groupers Did Not Do

I have found no evidence that the East Coast early A.A./Oxford Group meetings and house-parties that Bill, Lois, and others regularly attended involved the immense stress on Bible study that was evident in Akron. I have found no evidence that the Oxford Group's work of Moral Re-Armament (whatever its prior names) resembled the Christian Endeavor program. I have found clear evidence from Bill's own recorded statements that Bill had simply never even read, let alone studied, the Bible before he joined the Smiths and the non-alcoholics in Akron. I have found no particular emphasis in Oxford Group writings on the Book of James, the Sermon on the Mount, and 1 Corinthians 13–though it is fair to say that both the Bible and the foregoing Bible segments were at least known to, and frequently read by, East Coast Groupers (particularly its leaders like Reg. Sam Shoemaker and Rev. W. Irving Harris). I have seen no evidence that Bill Wilson, before he came to Akron, or even after he left, talked much about the Bible, the Creator, Jesus Christ, James, the Sermon, or Corinthians. Nor did he talk much, if at all, about Anne Smith's Journal or the extensive Christian literature A.A. pioneers read in Akron .Nor that he made any significant references to the devotionals–*The Upper Room, My Utmost for His Highest, The Runner's Bible*, or the books of Chambers, E. Stanley Jones, Fosdick, Clark, and others–that were in wide circulation in Akron..

New York A.A.'s Oxford Group Departure in 1937

Lois Wilson said that the "Oxford Group kind of kicked us out," and that she and Bill were not considered "maximum" by the groupers (*Pass It On*, p. 174). The two of them left the Oxford Group in August, 1937. Bill's connection with the Oxford Group and its meetings lasted only from about November, 1934 to August, 1937–though Bill and Lois had attended many meetings, gone to house-parties, met people like Dr. Frank Buchman, and spoken frequently about Oxford Group principles and practices. Bill *was* intensely involved with Oxford Group team events in New York in late 1935 and early 1936. After his departure, Bill developed a laundry list of reasons for the split with the Oxford Group (*Pass It On*, pp. 171-173). Yet he continued to be in close touch with Oxford Group leader Rev. Sam Shoemaker from 1934 until the end of Shoemaker's life. See Dick B., *New Light on Alcoholism: God, Sam Shoemaker, and A.A.*, 2d ed.

There is little doubt today that almost every idea in Wilson's Twelve Steps had its roots in Shoemaker's teachings (See Dick B., *Twelve Steps for You; New Light on Alcoholism: God, Sam Shoemaker, and A.A.*, as well as A.A.'s own *Alcoholics Anonymous Comes of Age*, p. 39, and *The Language of the Heart*, p. 298). But depart from the Oxford Group New York A.A. did. At the very least, the split can be ascribed to the highly critical attitudes and resultant departure of both Bill and Lois in 1937. Also to the ever-present Roman Catholic hostility to the Oxford Group and its "Buchmanism" (*Pass It On.*, p. 173; Dick B., *New Light on Alcoholism*, pp. 179-181, 401-420). Finally to the evident and presently expanding "universalization" of A.A.'s religious prototype in early years "since [as Lois Wilson put it] all drunks were not Christian" (*Lois Remembers*, p. 113; Dick B. *New Light on Alcoholism*, p. 177). Append to these three major points Bill's *ex post facto* laundry list of objections, if you like; but all sounded the death knell and put an end to the association of the Oxford Group and East Coast A.A..

The Limited Akron/Oxford Group Connection from the Beginning

The following discussion may not set well with those who have recently magnified the A.A./Oxford Group link seemingly with a *sub silencio* motive of criticizing A.A.'s real Biblical roots and Protestant orientation while really trying to pull down the Oxford Group, Frank Buchman, Moral Re-Armament, and then A.A. itself on every conceivable front. (See as examples; Ken Ragge, *The Real AA: Behind the Myth of 12-Step Recovery*, Martin and Deidre Bobgan, *12 Steps to Destruction*, Ernest Kurtz, *The Collected Ernie Kurtz*). These writers and some others seem frightened to death that some unsuspecting scholar, book publisher, or alcoholic might actually discover that A.A. had many many roots. Consequently, it is disingenuous for such writers to be talking down early A.A. religious ideas on the one hand, and, on the other, pick a controversial root like the Oxford Group as exemplifying A.A., and then shooting down the straw man.

Ironically, though it was an Oxford Group connection that brought Bill and Bob together, it was not, particularly Oxford Group enthusiasm. Lois didn't really care for most Oxford Group ideas at all, stating for example that she didn't need a "conversion" and "soul surgery." Bill did not like the Four Absolutes, with their insistence on purity. Bob did.favor those absolutes as "yardsticks" and said so during his entire A.A. association. Wilson did not like "soul-surgery." But Akron writers at least understood the concept. Bill had soon turned his own Oxford Group meetings into a search for drunks. Bob had not latched on to witnessing and outreach.

Bill, according to some, had never read any Oxford Group literature (and I found none of significance in his library at Stepping Stones). But Bob had read about everything they had to offer, and so had Henrietta and T. Henry Williams and probably Anne Smith and Clarace Williams. After leaving Akron in 1935, Bill did immediately and briefly associate himself with Oxford Group businessmen's team (though Lois did not join him). He also participated in Buchman's "world-changing" ideas in New York and Oxford Group houseparties, with Lois also in attendance. Bob did not. Bill never seemed willing–until many years after A.A.'s founding–to mention or admit the things he had borrowed for his Big Book and Steps from Shoemaker and the Group. Anne Smith discussed them at length in her workbook long before the Big Book was published. Henrietta used them in her meeting leads and in everyday life. T. Henry used them in the Akron surrenders and for the rest of his life. And Bob used them as a base for some of his work.

To be painfully frank, Oxford Group ideas influenced Bill Wilson at every turn including the language he put in his Big Book and Twelve Steps. But not so with Akron.

Akron began its alcoholic recovery experiments with the Bible. It urged reading of all kinds of Christian literature. It held old fashioned prayer meetings and group quiet times. It conducted the healing ministry of James. It marched into hospitals to help alcoholics. But Bill never gave any of these more than a nod except in his earliest sober period. Akron insisted on Christ. But Bill first treated Jesus with Oxford Group vagueness, and then soon left the Lord out of the picture entirely. Bill's wife justified the omission and universalization by saying, it was "because not all AAs are Christians." However, there is no evidence that Dr. Bob ever embraced such thinking. Bill sought world-wide outreach for A.A. after the manner of Buchman's world-changing. Dr. Bob seemed content to change drunks one-at-a-time, one-day-at-a-time, by bringing them to Christ and to reliance on the Creator. Dr. Bob liked his associations with Akron Oxford Group people he met and enjoyed their company while Bill's participation was pragmatic–how would his association help drunks. Bob called up his youthful experience in the church and Christian Endeavor. Bill had none to call on. Even Oxford Groupers in Akron suggested they were a "clandestine" Oxford Group lodge. This, it would seem, because their focus was on the Bible, on "old fashioned revival meetings," hospitalizations, helping drunks, reading Christian literature of all varieties, and using devotionals from many denominations as not typical of Oxford Group purposes and practices.

And this was not the way Bill Wilson utilized his Oxford Group activities.

A.A.'s connection with the Oxford Group via its Akron beginnings was far less significant and somewhat tenuous because of Akron's identifiable Christian Fellowship features and because of its insistent focus on helping alcoholics–in, into, and, wherever found–to total abstinence and early hospitalization.

Reasons for Akron's Departure

Akronites did not leave the Oxford Group because they were "kicked out." Nor did they leave because they didn't like the "Four Absolutes" or the "Five C's." Nor did they leave because they didn't like "conversion," didn't like "soul-surgery," didn't like Frank Buchman, or didn't like associating with a Christian Fellowship–all of which was totally unlike the position of the Wilsons, particularly Lois Wilson.

The reasons for Akron's departure are simply a matter of conjecture, based on diverse opinions. The earliest reason was that expressed by Clarence H. Snyder. Snyder was bringing several Roman Catholics drunks down from Cleveland to Akron for the Wednesday Oxford Group meetings. A Roman Catholic priest in Cleveland objected to their participation in what was a Protestant-oriented fellowship. Clarence asked Bob to let these people go to a new meeting in Cleveland, and Bob basically said they could take it or leave it in Akron. In fact, however, there were many Roman Catholic objections to the Oxford Group, and the tug on the Romans from Cleveland religious was heavy. So the Cleveland alcoholics formed the first all-alcoholic group. It was in Cleveland, and it was called "Alcoholics Anonymous." Bob, Henrietta, and some others attempted to stop the new effort, but they did not succeed. So, in Cleveland, A.A. left all connection with the Oxford Group behind though it long after referred to and used the Four Absolutes and the Bible. Co-incidentally, Cleveland A.A. - with its Big Book, Bible, and Four Absolutes--grew faster than any other group in the United States (a fact that Wilson himself publicly acknowledged at A.A.'s 25th Anniversary Conference in St. Louis).

Additional reasons for Akron's departure might have been that the T. Henry Williams home had grown too small for meetings; and they were briefly moved to Dr. Bob's Home and then to Akron's King School. Also, Dr. Bob shortly thereafter teamed up with Sister Ignatia to start hospitalizing and working with drunks at St. Thomas Hospital; and the

Roman Catholic objections to an Oxford Group program (openly mentioned by Sister Ignatia) were still clouding the background. Further, the Roman Church itself had seemed to foster a new distinction that was supposed to make A.A. palatable to all–rather than just those in Bible study, prayer-meeting, fellowships. The idea was that "religion" was for the church while "spirituality" was for A.A. And some of the earliest proponents of this "spiritual but not religious" crowd seem to have come from the Roman Catholic community. That distinction without a difference was pushed heavily, and it has become a touchstone today for all sorts of "spiritual" stuff in 12 Step programs that has nothing to do with the original religious character of A.A. But that rationale left Roman Catholics free to stay with their church for "religion" while free to "stop drinking" in A.A. with its "spiritual" program–whatever that meant then or means now. And you still hear it with frequency in A.A. meetings: "I go to my church for 'religion' and to A.A. for 'spirituality' and sobriety." This nonsense remark is commonplace in A.A. meetings today.

Some in the Akron A.A. fellowship remained with the Oxford Group after Cleveland A.A. was formed. Bob, Anne, and Henrietta remained friends with T. Henry and Clarace; and all the Akron pioneer members seemed saddened by the break. But the previous break in New York was clear and final The break in Cleveland was clear and final. And the finality was perhaps clinched by a sort of "treaty" made between Bob and Bill. According to Bill, the two men agreed that Bob was to focus on hospitalization and newcomer outreach–which he did. Bill was to focus on organization and growth–which he did. And that certainly left no room for the Oxford Group at all, especially after the three-fold departures in New York, Cleveland, and then Akron.

7

Let Go, and Let God

Henrietta Seiberling had an unflinching love for God and for others. She had an unwavering belief that God could heal the alcoholic and deliver him from the curse of alcoholism. She had compassion for those "medically incurable" "real" alcoholics who found their way into the fledgling Akron experiment that began in 1935. She believed that their freedom depended on their finding and relying on the power of the one, true, living God whose healing, forgiving, redeeming qualities are so clearly laid out in the Bible.

Her convictions were shared by the first A.A. group in Akron. This faith in God's "power-produced" cures astonished the world as the Akron experiment, successes, and cures became known and widely publicized. The news of the cures was trumpeted in A.A. for a decade.
There are hundreds of news articles that spoke of the cure of alcoholism and the A.A. members who specifically said they had been "cured." A.A.'s headquarters has scrapbooks with these "cured" articles; but almost every A.A. has never seen a one.

Then the lady with a cause perceived a shift in the A.A. Society from the simple convictions and program that were hammered out by the Akron pioneers. She attended meetings where she thought she was listening more to a discussion of psychiatry than to testimonies of the healing power of the Creator. And she said so. After Dr. Bob died, she clung to the ranks of those pioneers who still remembered, still believed, and still spoke of the power of the "One" in whom they had believed–Almighty God.

As the numbers of alcoholics in the Society increased in America to a million or more, their drop-out rate plummeted to ninety-nine percent, represented peopled in large part by those who left within a year. Early A.A.'s success rate of 75% to 93%–documented in the rosters which were kept, the pictures on the wall at Dr. Bob's Home, and the memories of pioneers–slipped to somewhere between 1 and 5 %.

The power of God was still available. It still is. And Ohio's non-alcoholic Henrietta knew what could be done by reliance on it. She continued to hold and espouse her belief. And, over the years, thousands in and outside of Akron have truly been able to count on their Creator, to "let go and let God," and experience His healing power, His guidance, His forgiveness, and the everlasting and abundant life He made available to believers through the death and resurrection of His son. (As to that everlasting life and that abundant life, see John 3:16 and John 10:10) The reliance and result are summed up in the motto seen on the walls of many A.A. fellowship rooms. The motto offers hope to those who want to believe. Fittingly, the motto is also inscribed on Henrietta's gravestone in Kentucky. The motto is Let Go, and Let God.

Let Go, and Let God: It is still an option for those who believe.

End

About the Author

Dick B. writes books on the spiritual roots of Alcoholics Anonymous. They show how the basic and highly successful biblical ideas used by early AAs can be valuable tools for success in today's A.A. His research can also help the religious and recovery communities work more effectively with alcoholics, addicts, and others involved in Twelve Step programs.

The author is an active, recovered member of A.A.; a retired attorney; and a Bible student. He has sponsored more than one hundred men in their recovery from alcoholism. Consistent with A.A.'s traditions of anonymity, he uses the pseudonym "Dick B."

He has had twenty-eight titles published including: *Dr. Bob and His Library*; *Anne Smith's Journal, 1933-1939*; *The Oxford Group & Alcoholics Anonymous*; *The Akron Genesis of Alcoholics Anonymous*; *The Books Early AAs Read for Spiritual Growth*; *New Light on Alcoholism: God, Sam Shoemaker, and A.A.*; *Courage to Change* (with Bill Pittman); *Cured: Proven Help for Alcoholics and Addicts; The Good Book and The Big Book: A.A.'s Roots in the Bible*; *That Amazing Grace: The Role of Clarence and Grace S. in Alcoholics Anonymous*; *Good Morning!: Quiet Time, Morning Watch, Meditation, and Early A.A.*; *Turning Point: A History of Early A.A.'s Spiritual Roots and Successes, Hope!: The Story of Geraldine D., Alina Lodge & Recovery; Utilizing Early A.A.'s Spiritual Roots for Recovery Today; The Golden Text of A.A.; By the Power of God; God and Alcoholism; Making Known the Biblical History of A.A.; Why Early A.A. Succeeded*; *Comments of Dick B. at The First Nationwide A.A. History Conference; Henrietta Seiberling: Ohio's Lady with a Cause;* and *The James Club*. The books have been the subject of newspaper articles and reviews in *Library Journal, Bookstore Journal, The Living Church, Faith at Work, Sober Times, Episcopal Life, Recovery News, Ohioana Quarterly, The PHOENIX,* and *The Saint Louis University Theology Digest.* They are listed in the biographies of major addiction center, religion, and religious history sites. He has published over 150 articles on his subject, most posted on the internet.

Dick is the father of two sons (Ken and Don) and has two granddaughters. As a young man, he did a stint as a newspaper reporter. He attended the University of California, Berkeley, where he received his A.A. degree with Honorable Mention, majored in economics, and was elected to Phi Beta Kappa in his Junior year. In the United States Army, he was an Information-Education Specialist. He received his A.B. and J.D. degrees from Stanford University, and was Case Editor of the Stanford Law Review. Dick became interested in Bible study in his childhood Sunday School and was much inspired by his mother's almost daily study of Scripture. He joined, and was president of, a Community Church affiliated with the United Church of Christ. By 1972, he was studying the origins of the Bible and began traveling abroad in pursuit of that subject. In 1979, he became much involved in a Biblical research, teaching, and fellowship ministry. In his community life, he was president of a merchants' council, Chamber of Commerce, church retirement center, and homeowners' association. He served on a public district board and has held offices in a service club.

In 1986, he was felled by alcoholism, gave up his law practice, and began recovery as a member of the Fellowship of Alcoholics Anonymous. In 1990, his interest in A.A.'s Biblical/Christian roots was sparked by his attendance at A.A.'s International Convention in Seattle. He has traveled widely; researched at archives, and at public and seminary libraries; interviewed scholars, historians, clergy, A.A. "old-timers" and survivors; and participated in programs and conferences on A.A.'s roots.

The author is the owner of Good Book Publishing Company and has several works in progress. Much of his research and writing is done in collaboration with his older son, Ken, an ordained minister, who holds B.A., B.Th., and M.A. degrees. Ken has been a lecturer in New Testament Greek at a Bible college and a lecturer in Fundamentals of Oral Communication at San Francisco State University. Ken is a computer specialist and director of marketing and research in Hawaii ethanol projects.

Dick is a member of the American Historical Association, Research Society on Alcoholism, Alcohol and Drugs History Society, Organization of American Historians, The Association for Medical Education and Research in Substance Abuse, Coalition of Prison Evangelists, Christian Association for Psychological Studies, and International Substance Abuse and Addictions Coalition. He is available for conferences, panels, seminars, and interviews.

Good Book Publishing Company Order Form

(Use this form to order Dick B.'s titles on early A.A.'s roots and successes)

Qty.	Titles by Dick B.	Price	
____	*A New Way In*	$19.95 ea. $	______
____	*A New Way Out*	$19.95 ea. $	______
____	*Anne Smith's Journal, 1933-1939*	$22.95 ea. $	______
____	*By the Power of God: A Guide to Early A.A. Groups and Forming Similar Groups Today*	$23.95 ea. $	______
____	*Cured! Proven Help for Alcoholics and Addicts*	$23.95 ea. $	______
____	*Dr. Bob and His Library*	$22.95 ea. $	______
____	*Dr. Bob of Alcoholics Anonymous*	$24.95 ea. $	______
____	*God and Alcoholism*	$21.95 ea. $	______
____	*Good Morning! Quiet Time, Morning Watch, Meditation, and Early A.A.*	$22.95 ea. $	______
____	*Henrietta B. Seiberling*	$20.95 ea. $	______
____	*Introduction to the Sources and Founding of A.A.*	$22.95 ea. $	______
____	*Making Known the Biblical History and Roots of Alcoholics Anonymous*	$24.95 ea. $	______
____	*New Light on Alcoholism: God, Sam Shoemaker, and A.A.*	$24.95 ea. $	______
____	*Real Twelve Step Fellowship History*	$23.95 ea. $	______
____	*That Amazing Grace: The Role of Clarence and Grace S. in Alcoholics Anonymous*	$22.95 ea. $	______
____	*The Akron Genesis of Alcoholics Anonymous*	$23.95 ea. $	______
____	*The Books Early AAs Read for Spiritual Growth*	$21.95 ea. $	______
____	*The Conversion of Bill W.*	$23.95 ea. $	______
____	*The First Nationwide A.A. History Conference*	$22.95 ea. $	______
____	*The Golden Text of A.A.*	$20.95 ea. $	______
____	*The Good Book and the Big Book: A.A.'s Roots in the Bible*	$23.95 ea. $	______
____	*The Good Book-Big Book Guidebook*	$22.95 ea. $	______
____	*The James Club and the Original A.A. Program's Absolute Essentials*	$23.95 ea. $	______
____	*The Oxford Group and Alcoholics Anonymous*	$23.95 ea. $	______
____	*Turning Point: A History of Early A.A.'s Spiritual Roots and Successes*	$29.95 ea. $	______
____	*Twelve Steps for You*	$21.95 ea. $	______
____	*Utilizing Early A.A.'s Spiritual Roots for Recovery Today*	$20.95 ea. $	______
____	*When Early AAs Were Cured and Why*	$23.95 ea. $	______
____	*Why Early A.A. Succeeded*	$23.95 ea. $	______

(Order Form continued on the next page)

Good Book Publishing Company Order Form

(continued from the previous page)

Order Subtotal: $ ______

Shipping and Handling (S&H) **: $ ______

(** For Shipping and Handling, please add 10% of the Order Subtotal for U.S. orders or 15% of the Order Subtotal for international orders. The minimum U.S. S&H is $5.60. The minimum S&H for Canada and Mexico is US$ 9.95. The minimum S&H for other countries is US$ 11.95.)

Order Total: $ ______

Credit card: VISA MasterCard American Express Discover (circle one)

Account number: ____ Exp.: ______

Name: __________________________________ (as it is on your credit card, if using one)

(Company: ____)

Address Line 1: ____

Address Line 2: ____

City: _______________________________________ State/Prov.: ____________

Zip/Postal Code: _______________ Country: ____________________________

Signature: ____________________________ Telephone: ____________________

Email: ____

No returns accepted. Please mail this Order Form, along with your check or money order (if sending one), to: Dick B., c/o Good Book Publishing Company, PO Box 837, Kihei, HI 96753-0837. Please make your check or money order (if sending one) payable to "Dick B." in U.S. dollars drawn on a U.S. bank. If you have any questions, please phone: 1-808-874-4876 or send an email message to: dickb@dickb.com. Dick B.'s web site: www.DickB.com.

If you would like to purchase Dick B.'s entire 29-volume reference set on early A.A.'s roots and successes (and how those successes may be replicated today) at a substantial discount, please send Dick B. an email message or give him a call.

Paradise Research Publications, Inc.
PO Box 837
Kihei, HI 96753-0837
(808) 874-4876
Email: dickb@dickb.com
URL: http://www.dickb.com/index.shtml
http://www.dickb-blog.com

Made in the USA
Monee, IL
04 November 2026

67384323R00049